Fame, many possessions,
good reputation cannot
go with you
when you die.

Open, Breath, Love
Compassion, humility
patience, non-attachment
to worldly things
gratitutude, emptiness —
all is empty

By Judd Apatow:

Sick in the Head

I Found This Funny

IT'S GARRY SHANDLING'S BOOK

IT'S GARRY SHANDLING'S BOOK

Edited by Judd Apatow

Random House
New York

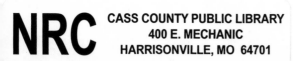

Published in the United States by Random House, an imprint and division of Penguin Random House LLC, New York.

RANDOM HOUSE and the HOUSE colophon are registered trademarks of Penguin Random House LLC.

Grateful acknowledgment is made to The Maynard Dixon Museum, Tucson, AZ, for permission to reprint a handwritten copy and transcription of the poem "Sanctuary" by Maynard Dixon. Used by permission.

LIBRARY OF CONGRESS CATALOGING-IN-PUBLICATION DATA
Names: Shandling, Garry, author. | Apatow, Judd, editor.
Title: It's Garry Shandling's book / edited by Judd Apatow.
Description: First edition. | New York: Random House, [2019] | Includes bibliographical references. |
Identifiers: LCCN 2019027874 (print) | LCCN 2019027875 (ebook) |
ISBN 9780525510840 (hardcover) | ISBN 9780525510857 (ebook)
Subjects: LCSH: Shandling, Garry. | Comedians—United States—Biography. | Jewish comedians—United States—Biography. | Actors—United States—Biography.
Classification: LCC PN2287.S358 A3 2019 (print) | LCC PN2287.S358 (ebook) | DDC 792.702/8092 [B]—dc23
LC record available at https://lccn.loc.gov/2019027874
LC ebook record available at https://lccn.loc.gov/2019027875

Printed in China on acid-free paper

randomhousebooks.com

Text research and selection: Keith Staskiewicz

Layout and design: Bill Smith/designSimple

Case design: Ben Wiseman
Front-case photograph: Mark Seliger
Back-case photographs: NBC/Getty Images (Shandling in black & white); Bonnie Schiffman (Shandling popping out of TV); Garry Shandling Estate (Shandling touching shoes; Shandling pointing fingers)

9 8 7 6 5 4 3 2 1

First Edition

CONTENTS

The Larry Sanders Show
DIRECTOR: JUDD APATOW
CAMERA: PETER SMOKLER
DATE: 2 / 28 / 98   EPISODE #609

INTRODUCTION

By Judd Apatow

When Garry died suddenly we were all lost. I am a hoarder. I try to hold on to everything. My first instinct was to hoard Garry. He had always been my mentor, my friend, and my greatest inspiration in creativity and life. He was not a perfect man, but he was always trying to reach the next level. When I was a young man he handed me a Buddhist book called *Catching a Feather on a Fan*, and it brought spirituality into my life for the first time. I dealt with this loss by refusing to let go of any of Garry. I am pretty sure that goes against all of the tenets of Buddhism.

Garry had a large home that he built himself and was never entirely comfortable in. The joke with his friends was how he always complained about it. He would hire people to draw up designs about how to fix it, and then would never like them enough to actually move forward. When I entered his house to help deal with his material possessions, I wondered what I would find. He never seemed like the kind of person who kept anything. I didn't see him as sentimental. I remember one year, way before streaming, I got him every episode of *Inside the Actors Studio* on VHS for his birthday. As I handed it to him, I realized he would never watch it and wondered what black hole it would disappear into.

When I first went through his office it seemed like there wasn't much to deal with, barely a personal photo. All of his awards were in a trophy case he had built next to his washer and dryer. He had a loft above an office next to his garage that had some boxes from his TV-series days.

It felt like he was living his Buddhist life, not holding on to the past, trying to live in the moment. Then I opened a closet and found a stack of boxes. I soon realized that Garry kept everything. He seemed to just chuck items into boxes, then put them in closets and never look at them again. I opened one and found a box of letters Garry had written to his college-era girlfriend. Someone told me that after she died, her parents sent them to Garry. I opened another box and found letters to his parents, his earliest joke notebooks, and reel-to-reel tapes of a young Garry performing his earliest stand-up act alone into a tape recorder.

It went on and on, box after box. His house had no family photos displayed, but there was a box of hundreds of childhood photographs perfectly preserved.

The most important find was a trunk that contained all of his journals since 1978. I quietly debated whether or not I should read them. Twenty seconds later I started reading them. I was afraid I would lose respect for him if I knew all his secrets and deepest feelings. What I discovered was that he was an even better person than I had realized. Decade after decade I just read about a man struggling to figure out how to be more open and loving. There were some details about conflicts with friends, girlfriends, and work associates, but the vast majority of his writings were reminders to himself about the man he wanted to be. In his private thoughts he would constantly remind himself to let go of his ego and to seek evolution as a person. He also had a lot of amazing jokes, many of which never saw the light of day.

In the years before his death he had considered projects that would be based on these journals. I took that as meaning that Garry knew there was wisdom in his journey, which he wanted to share with others. People who have seen our documentary, *The Zen Diaries of Garry Shandling*, told me how impactful his diary entries were to them. Some even took photos of the screen.

This book is the final major Garry Shandling project. I am very honored to be a part of excavating photos, jokes, journals, script pages, interviews, and anything that I thought would help illuminate this fascinating, brilliant, and kind man. This is the ultimate hoarding of Garry. I hope you enjoy it.

IT'S GARRY SHANDLING'S BOOK

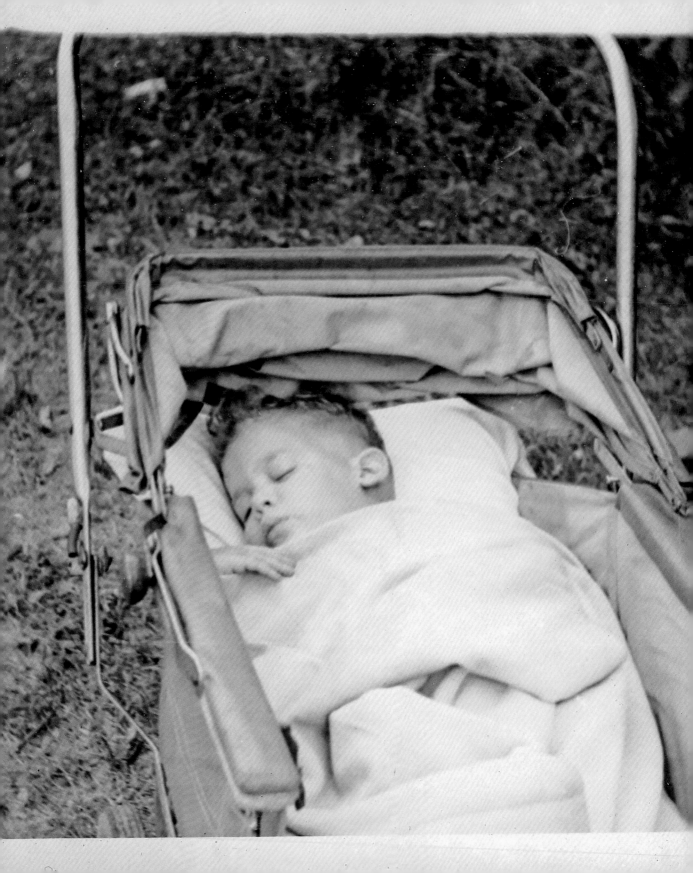

THE ONLY JEW IN TUCSON

In his first of many debuts, Garry Shandling arrived on November 29, 1949, in a Chicago hospital room to parents Irv and Muriel Shandling.

GARRY Only Donald Trump knows what's on my birth certificate. It says Garry—two *r*'s—Emmanuel Shandling. And then under sex it says, "See long form."

The Only Jew in Tuscon

I was born in of a Chicago. And I had a very slight case of astma, my folks said maybe we should move to Arizona. I said " just Vacuum!! "

1983

GARRY I might have been manic had they lived in New York. But they were in Chicago and moved to Arizona when I was two. So I grew up in the desert. I was the only Jew. I mean, the "Don't ask, don't tell" applied to me for fifteen years. I didn't say jack shit. I'd say, "No, no, I wasn't celebrating the holiday. I had a cold."

MIKE SHANDLING (Garry's cousin) Garry was born in Chicago. Maybe he was six months old at the time, sometime in the middle of 1950. They moved to Tucson because Garry's older brother, Barry, had cystic fibrosis, so it was more for his health purposes to go down there, and that's pretty much where he grew up. So he's a Tucson kid. I'm his first cousin. Our fathers were brothers. Garry's dad was Irving, and my dad was Barney Shandling. And there were two sisters, Irene and May.

I grew up in Tucson, Arizona, where it's, like, 120 degrees in the summer. One day our dog ran by and just burst into flames.

RENE - MURIEL

MURIEL JRV 1944

MURIEL   IRV   BARNEY   LOIS

GARRY   BARRY · MIKE · DEB

GARRY My dad owned a big printing company. Lithography company. He had, like, three presses, and he did all the books for the University of Arizona. Sort of a noted printer within the printing industry.

She owned a pet shop. My mother was a little . . . special, a little loopy. She had her name above the pet shop. So it was the Animal Fair Pet Shop in a strip mall in Tucson, but it said "Muriel Shandling's Animal Fair," like the name above the title of a movie if you're a big star. You know, if you think about it, you usually don't see the person's name who's the owner above the name of the store you're going into. Except for Ralph's. My mom was humorous in a way that was unintended, and my father had a kind of a dry wit. But not overtly funny really.

My mom raised parrots. In fact she never tucked me in. She just put a towel over my head.

GARRY I actually gave my mom a really nice thank-you gift for her birthday once. And wrote a note on there saying, "Mom, I couldn't have done this without you, thank you." And she looked at it—this is true—and then took a beat, and then looked up—we were alone in the kitchen—and she said, "Why can't you say this on TV?" And I looked at her, and I said, "Let me see if I have this right: Would it mean more to you if I said it on TV as opposed to right now when I'm with you, in the kitchen, in person, speaking to you as your son?" She said, "On TV." And that's true.

Too the best
Mother in the
World!

Dear Mother
I hope you
never overwork.
For if yoo did
you would go be zerk.
And that is why you
deserve a trophy
for your work.

LOV
Gary

DEC 55

BARRY & GARRY

The Only Jew in Tuscon

GARRY I had a brother who died when I was ten. He was thirteen. He had cystic fibrosis, which is a lung disease. So while I was born in Chicago, we moved to Tucson because it's a dry heat. Unlike the Miami Heat. I always thought the Phoenix team should have been called the Dry Heat. But they chose the Suns.

MIKE SHANDLING Cystic fibrosis is a disease of the lungs, and it maybe involves the pancreas also. It creates a lot of fluid in the lungs, and at that time, it was a disease that you didn't make it much past thirteen years old. So the prognosis was never that Barry was gonna live a long fruitful life. It was probably more certain that he wouldn't get much past twelve or thirteen years old. So they knew that all along.

We did as much as he could do, and if he had to go and sit down or stop, we would continue playing. It didn't stop us from doing our thing, and Barry would do as much as he could do. There would be, not benefits, but collections. We would go to the drive-in movie theater and stand with collection cans outside the snack bar for donations, "Help cystic fibrosis" and stuff. So we were pretty aware and involved with it in Tucson. There were a lot of kids like him. Tucson seemed to be a place that if you had asthma or cystic fibrosis or things like that, it was a great place to go 'cause it was healthy, dry air.

They were close. They were always close, even from early on. Barry was his big brother, and Barry took care of Garry, really, was always protecting him and shielding him, and Garry, especially younger, would follow Barry around. But they were pretty close. It came to the point that he had so much trouble breathing that he really couldn't be active, and so became bedridden and had to stay in an oxygen tent, for obvious reasons, because his lungs were so full of fluid. I wanna say it's between the last three to six months. He wasn't able to be up and running around, and it was just a sad time for Garry and all of us. I think we knew that he wasn't gonna get better. They didn't try and sugarcoat that.

The thing I remember in our family as kids growing up is when the parents did things, they didn't really involve the kids in the discussions. All through my childhood, when there was serious stuff to talk about, we didn't really know what was going on. I just remember it was quiet and not much was really said after that. Sort of odd to me that it just seems like, poof, Barry was gone and that was it.

All these years, we never talked about Barry. Never again. I just think it was probably painful for him, and it's a childhood pain that just gets suppressed down in there and you just don't wanna bring it up. Because of the pain involved in it. I don't think Garry ever stopped thinking about Barry or loving him. He was in his heart. I just don't think he ever had the desire to talk about it. It had to be really tough for him. But on the other hand they made sure there was a lot of love that they were showering him with, and I think that probably also maybe started some of the issues with Muriel too, because she lost her oldest child. And Garry's all she has left and so now she's going to protect him and be hovering over him.

Garry reflects on his brother's
death decades later, in 2005.

Before Mother, you were
a happy boy in your
body. His death
was a mind - fuck
event, you and disappointment
you had to deal with
on your own. Go
back into body, and
don't try to avoid
pain.

It is a struggle to
to stay in the body,
for everyone. Discipline,
Breathing Confusion
into a coping mechanism.

2005

United States Army
Military Affiliate Radio System
STATION LICENSE

A D 7 B K G

GARRY E. SHANDLING   has agreed to operate the

The licensee, Radio Station licensed herein in accordance with all the governing
rules and regulations now or hereafter prescribed by the Chief, Military
Affiliate Radio System, Department of the Army.

By Authority of the Secretary of the Army

George E. Pickett
Major General, GS
Assistant Chief of Staff for
Communications-Electronics

Issued at Washington, D.C.   August 20 1968

This license shall remain valid until June 15 1970
unless sooner modified or revoked for cause.

WA7BKG was Garry's first call sign as a licensed ham radio operator. The initials in the lower left corner stand for his affiliated organizations: Old Pueblo Radio Club, American Radio Relay League, and the Rag Chewers' Club.

MIKE SHANDLING Garry was really into ham radio, and I think he started probably at twelve or thirteen, and that was what he did in his spare time. All his friends were ham radio guys, and he had people all around the world that were his ham radio friends. Ham radio, you could talk to people anywhere in the world. He could talk to people in Japan. He could talk to people in Australia. Places that you only saw in books and school. And he had friends all over the world that he never met but he talked to. I think

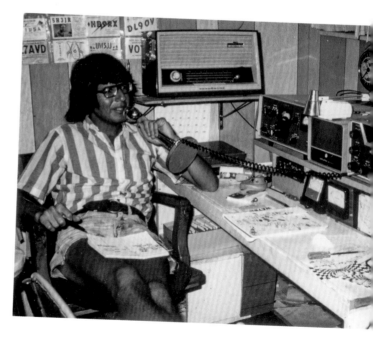

Garry, at that point, became a little introverted. And I don't know if it was a reaction to Barry passing, or if it was the fact that he was more of an electronic engineering nerd, for lack of a better term. I mean, he was into it. He had all the best equipment and latest equipment and was always letting us sit with him for hours and hours, just talking on the ham radio.

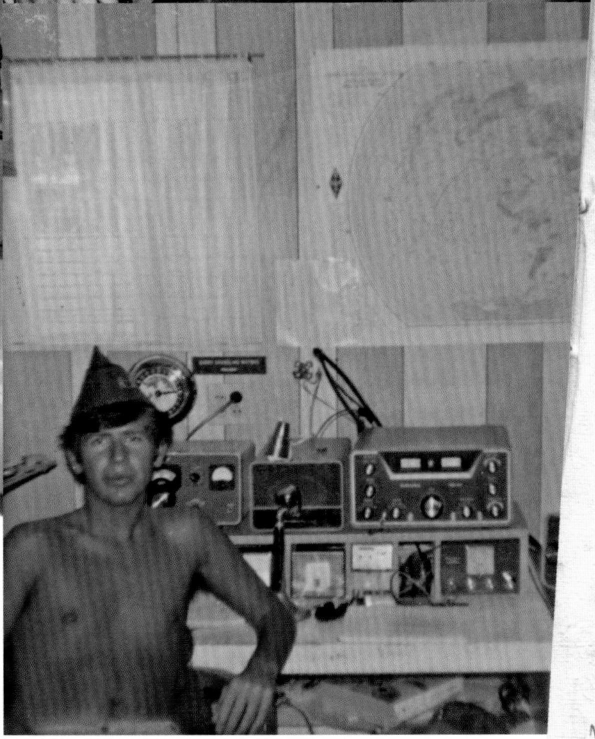

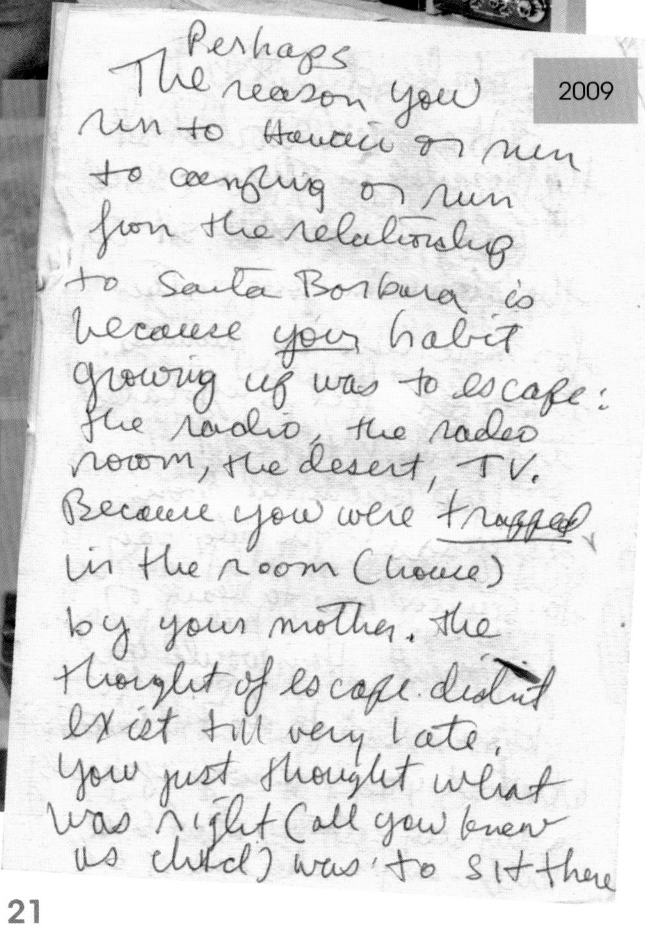

2009

Perhaps
The reason you
run to Hawaii or run
to camping or run
from the relationship
to Santa Barbara is
because your habit
growing up was to escape:
the radio, the radio
room, the desert, TV.
Because you were trapped
in the room (house)
by your mother, the
thought of escape didn't
exist till very late.
You just thought what
was right (all you knew
as child) was to sit there

21

See, You Hold Them Like This
Hiroki Shioji, 19, of Wakayama City, Japan, explains the use of chop sticks to Garry Shandling, 15. The Japanese boy will enter the University of Arizona this fall as another chapter in a strange story that began as a pen pal exchange five years ago. (Sheaffer photo by Mark Godfrey)

Both Stamp Collectors 537

Pen Pals Triumph Over Difficulties

Japanese Youth Arrive In Tucson, Joins Friend; Enters School On Scholarship

By LARRY FERGUSON

A pen pal friendship that began in March, 1959, between Tucson and Wakayama City, Japan collectors entered a new chapter this week as Hiroki Shioji, 19, joined the Irving Shandling family, 6638 E. Calle de San Alberto.

The correspondence was started by Barry Shandling on the basis of a mutual interest in stamp collecting. But the warm friendship that developed as letters crisscrossed the Pacific was shattered by Barry's death in Jan. 1960, of cystic fibrosis. He was 13 years old.

GARRY When I was growing up, we had a foreign student from Japan staying at our house named Hiroki. And he actually took Japanese in college in order to get good grades. Can you imagine being in that class when they call roll and they call "Hiroki Shioji"? And he goes, "Here." And everybody goes, "Oh, shit. There goes the curve."

We had a lot of foreign students staying with us. My mom made kids from fifty different countries neurotic. Hiroki was walking around saying, "Oh, I have big problems. How's my hair?"

Wakayama City.
May 9, 1963

Dear Garry,

      Thank you for your pleasing letter and many stamps.
I hardly can wait for the tape from you!! I have been dreaming about what you spoke about for me! And I am sure that it
is very good, useful, interesting thing for us to send the
tapes. Especially, as for me, whenever I listen to the tapes
carefully and delightedly, they will help me to brush up my
poor English.

    By the way, about the nuclear powered submarine disaster,
yes, you are right; we are so sorry to hear it, we have oft-
en heard about that of Thresher and we all have been deeply
shocked.
    But when we think of the Telstar II, we are very glad, for
the world-wide telecast will soon be realized with many communication satellites as Telstar: it is no longer a dream,is it?

    Lt. Col. John H. Glenn Jr., the first American astronaut as
you told me, arrived in Japan early Sunday morning to coope-
rate in another U.S. space flight around the middle of this
month and Maj. Gordon Cooper is the astronaut of this time,
I hear. If I remember right Col. Glenn orbited the earth three times in the spaceship Friendship 7 on February 21 last
year.
    So it is very good timing to listen to his conversation
with the tape you sent me during his stay in Japan.

    I suppose it may be difficult for me English as a second
language to understand the conversation between Col. Glenn
and the controller on the earth and what the announcer says
for they speak difficult words for us with rapidity. But if
it should be difficult to understand them, I will do my best
to understand them as well as your words.

                    Sincerely yours,

                    Hiroki

A pen-pal letter from Hiroki.

I was kind of wimpy in high school.
I was beaten up a lot. I was actually
deboned in the seventh grade.

Dick Sch...ikert
Craig Scott
Ch... Seipelt
...ristine Sewell
Timothy Sewell
James Shaffery
Bob Shallenberger

Garry Shandling
Charlotte Shaver
Bob Shaw
Miles Shaw
Mark Shaydak
Kris Shelton
Alice Shockley

Debby Shoemake
...rn Shupe
Ju... Sibley
Wally Sidebottom
Bob Sil...
Juanita Simmon...
Ken Simms

Jerry Smart
Barbara Smith
Dia Smith
LaRee Smith
Sandi Smith
Stephanie Smith
Susan Smith

Walter Smith
Bobbie Smyth
Craig Soland
Linda Soldin
Karen Speaks
Gary Spence
Richard Spencer

Joan Spillman
Donna Spogen
Elaine Spoon
Jayne Stafford
Mona Stalcup
Danny Stanley
Ruth Staples

Opposite page: In an early bit of funny business, young Garry defines a "dipple."

The Only Jew in Tuscon

No Corrections OK

①

What is a dipple?

A dipple is a guy who tries to go down stairs on a skateboard.

A dipple is your best friend who says he's selling you a Beatle record and then you find out its "Buck Owens singing Hillbilly Heaven and other Country Music Hits."

A dipple is a guy who eats only the hole of the doughnut.

A dipple is a guy that flunks Physical Education for mental reasons.

A dipple is your girlfriend who sends you a valentine C.O.D.

A dipple is a guy who wears his right foot on his left shoe.

A dipple is a guy who thinks mouth to mouth resusitation is a type of water game.

A dipple is Cassius Clay.

A dipple is the freshman who has the locker under your and persists on cramming his head into your locker door when he stands up.

A dipple is a lady who just <u>won't believe</u> she's on Candid Camera.

A dipple is guy who watches "December Bride" reruns.

A dipple is a female driver education teacher.

A dipple is a guy whose fingers trip while they're walking through the yellow pages.

A dipple is a guy who feeds walnuts to monkeys.

A dipple is a guy who kills flys with "Right Guard" and uses "Black Flag" for deoderant.

A dipple is a guy who thinks a bagle is a type of dog.

A dipple is a guy that plays Chipmunk records at a slower speed just so he can hear what the voices <u>really sound like.</u>

A dipple is a guy that laughs at a dirty joke and then goes home to look up the words.

A dipple is a Muck.

A dipple is the guy who wears red and white on blue and gold day.

A dipple is a guy that does a jacknife off the diving board only to find he's in the shallow end.

Letter to 16 year old

1) Acne goes away. It's perhaps the biggest advantage to growing older. But then your hair thins, but don't think about that now.

2) Time doesn't actually exist. However, in this impermanent world, the illusion that time is passing is a sign that points to what some physicists call this relative word. You do not exist in as I write this. Nor do I, at this age, in your world. But, on another plane we are one, happening simultaneously,

5) Grow-up

6) I want to assure you that you are enough. Don't doubt this. It is You are just as God intended.

7) Learn to meditate

8) I will always be there to guide and give you advice.

9) Stop masturbating

10) One day you will not have to wear glasses, there is a surgery that can fix your eyes. I know how bad yours are. The doctor may have to go in thru the back.

GARRY I remember wanting to stay up late to watch Steve Allen and Jack Paar and those sorts of groundbreaking early talk shows. Otherwise sports. And I would watch *The Tonight Show* or *Ed Sullivan* or something and see comedians. I was fascinated with it in a way that I was sort of unaware of. Because I was shy, as most actually are, and one day in about eighth grade—seventh or eighth or ninth grade—I got up in front of class and did a Mel Brooks piece from his albums. And to me it's still astonishing that I would do that. I wouldn't do that now. I couldn't go to a seventh-grade class now and perform, for fear still that I would get beaten up after the class.

GARRY When I was a freshman in high school there was a kid—this is absolutely true—who committed suicide the day after the seating plan was announced. I still have this awful, sickening feeling that when he found out he was sitting next to me he just said, "I'd rather shoot myself."

The Only Jew in Tuscon

11) Be just who you are

12) Know the world is impermanent, and is in constant movement. Nothing, by nature, is ever exactly the same the next time

13) Punch a couple of kids at school. I can't recall their names now, but you know who I'm talking about:

14) Please don't wait till you're 22 to move out of the house / away from home.

I'm still choking / suffocated by it

5) iPod, DVD, HD, Blue tooth, No these aren't diseases. Or are they?

16) You think your ham radio set is fancy technology. Just Wait.

A letter Garry wrote to himself in 2010.

GARRY I was a funny kid, and I was always in trouble for talking in class. They would make me stay after school and pick weeds in the school yard as punishment. And by the fourth grade I was doing, like, the lawn and the hedges and everything. Eventually, they fired the maintenance crew. They said, "This kid's going to do it all!"

TUCSON PUBLIC SCHOOLS
Tucson, Arizona

First reporting period.   Date   January 24, 1956

Dear Mr. and Mrs. Shandling:

Garry has shown much growth in reading. He seems much more sure of
himself, and enjoys reading.

His writing still reflects immaturity in motor skills. He appears to
enjoy creative activities. He has shown marked improvement in independent
work. He is sometimes easily led into activities which he knows will get
him into trouble.

He enjoys working and playing with the other children and has become a
good member of the group. He sometimes needs reminding of his responsibilities,
but has also grown much in this respect.

I am enjoying very much working with Garry this year.

                                   Sincerely,

                                   Miss Johnson

Second reporting period.   Date   May 25, 1956

Dear Mr. and Mrs. Shandling:

Garry continues to show remarkable growth in his work. He seems to have gained
the needed time for achievement, and has matured beautifully in his school
situation. His reading has come along very nicely. His writing and creative
work shows growth, as well as interest and effort.

Garry's attitude has also shown growth. He seems to be more responsible and
cooperative than earlier. He has been a very nice child to work with and
I have enjoyed this year with him. I wish him much success in the years to come.

                                   Sincerely,

                                   Eleanor Johnson

Garry attended the University of Arizona from 1967 to 1971, but his most important lesson would end up taking place in a greenroom, not a classroom, with his work graded by one of the greatest comedy professors of all time.

COLLEGE, CARLIN, AND CAREERS

UNIVERSITY OF ARIZONA
IDENTIFICATION CARD—NON-TRANSFERABLE

Student's Signature

166875
Matriculation Number

Registrar

Spring - 1969

OLD MAIN

GARRY Once I got into college and met kids from New York, I realized there was a big difference in the frenetic energy pace that they possessed as opposed to mine, which was this very laid-back, desert-tortoise, I-really-shouldn't-walk-too-fast-because-the-sun-will-get-me attitude.

GARRY I never saw a comedian work live in a club until I was about twenty years old. Because I grew up in Tucson, Arizona, where there's just nothing. And I'd only seen comedians on TV. And then my folks used to go to Vegas when I was like thirteen, fourteen, fifteen, and I saw Joey Bishop and people like that. I actually remember knowing some of his jokes before he delivered them, and going, *Oh, man, he's doing old jokes.* Although he did a lot of original material as well, but I remember even being thirteen and going, *Oh, that's old*. So it was always an instinct for me. But to answer your question there, I didn't see a comedian till I was like twenty, in a club. I went to see George Carlin, who I'm just a major fan of.

GARRY I was an electrical engineering major seriously for three years. And one day I walked out of the lab. I was designing circuitry and I walked out to get some water and I couldn't walk back in. I just literally, like in a movie, just couldn't. And that's been a sort of model of what I have felt every time I've changed directions in

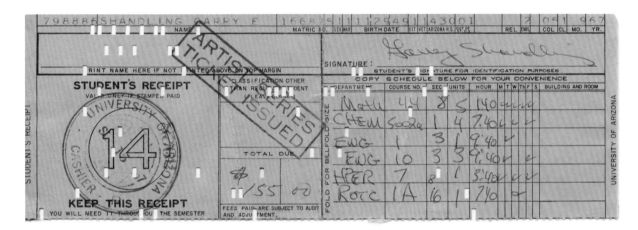

my career as I've moved along. At nineteen I had three years of engineering under my belt, which included Introduction to Atomic Physics and twenty-one units of math. It was a struggle to maintain a C average.

So there I was, unable to walk back into that class, and I thought, *I can't do this the rest of my life.* And I went home. I lived with my parents and I went into my bedroom. And I don't know what happened, but I sat down and I actually thought, *What am I going to do?* I was thinking about it and it struck me that, *Well, I like comedy.* And at that point in high school and so forth, I used to write funny essays and I'd read them in class—it was clear that I could write to some degree. So I thought, *This is what I like to do, and I seem to be able to learn.* I didn't think that I had any specific talent, or I didn't think that I had any gift, or that I automatically could do something.   (CONTINUED)

Garry Shandling
6638 Calle de San Alberto
Tucson, Arizona   85710   March 2, 1973

I don't want to say my secretary is dumb, but she thinks
National Guard is the name of a new spray deodorant.

Times are certainly changing. When I told a panhandler I
didn't have any spare change he told me he could take Bank Americard.

My secretary is so uncoordinated that her fingers trip while
walking through the yellow pages.

I come from a very Puritanical family. My mother wouldn't
even let me have an erector set because she thought it was
something dirty.

I read in the paper that a young activist called a policeman a
"pig," and was sentenced to spend three days in a pig sty. It's
a good thing he didn't call the cop a "smart ass"—who knows
where he would have had to spend his time.

My wife keeps telling me it was a good year when her mother was
born. She's right—her mother's a blimp.

All of the schools that teach sex education have ordered that
boys with mustaches must shave them off during the section on
oral sex in order to prevent any ticklish situations.

My mother's cooking was out of this world. I remember riding
my bike home from school I could smell the aroma a mile away:
mom was cooking dinner, or they were repaving the road again.

The government has finally revealed the secret weapon it used
to win the Vietnam conflict. They let Vice-president Agnew go over
there on a golfing holiday. He teed off in Saigon and played
through into Hanoi and poof! the war was over.

Some of Garry's earliest professional jokes.

I don't want to say my friend is straight, but I asked him to pass the joint and he gave me his elbow.

I told my girl friend that when I die I want to be buried on top of her so that when rigor mortis sets in, she'll get hers.

I just took a course in the new math, and like it was a real shock because for years I thought logarithm was a type of birth control.

My wife is on the chubby side. Actually, I'm not sure that "chubby" is the right word. Let me put it to you this way: when we cross a street in a cross-walk we have to go single file.

I ordered fresh salmon at the commissary this afternoon. And it was really fresh—right in the middle of the meal it tried to swim uptable.

I was going to go see "Last Tango in Paris," but I don't like musicals.

I get no respect; even the Avon lady rings the doorbell and then runs before I get a chance to answer it.

For my grandfather's 75th birthday we all chipped up and bought him an erector set. Which at his age consisted of a splint and a roll of masking tape.

It's not that my friend is dumb, but he put up a three foot redwood fence around his house and he's still waiting for it to grow.

To totally blow my confidence in flying, on my last flight the pilot announced on the P.A. system that the landing would be delayed because of the weather. He couldn't decide whether to land with the landing gear up or whether to land with the gear down.   (This line can be used with many subject matters as long as the pun on "weather" is utilized. The following line is an example.)

My wife wouldn't play golf with me last week on account of the weather. She couldn't decide whether to wear green slacks or whether to wear brown slacks.

MEN'S

Rampage, 3550 N. Lombard St.
Franklin Park, Ill. 60131. Editor:
Jack Steele. Sample for 25¢.

Penthouse Magazine, 1560 Broadway,
N.Y., N.Y. 10036. Editor: Edward
Ernest.

The Men's Digest, Best For Men,
2715 N. Pulaski Rd., Chicago, Ill.
60639. Editor: Frank Sorren.

Man To Man, Mr., Sir, 21 W. 26th
St. New York, N.Y. 10010. Editor:
Everett Meyers. JOKES ONLY

Male 625 Madison Ave. N.Y., N.Y. 10022
Editor: Carl Sifakis. JOKES ONLY

Esquire 488 Madison Ave. N.Y., N.Y.
10022. Editor: Harold Hayes.
Fiction: Julie Schwartz Asst. Editor

✱ Cavalier 236 East 46th St. N.Y. N.Y.
10017. Fiction Dept. Editor Maurice
De Walt.

Adam 8060 Melrose Ave. Los
Angeles Calif. 90046 Editor: Merrill
Miller

1967

But I thought I could learn—I had the ability to learn. I was a good student. And I thought, *What if I took that ability and applied it to something I like?* And I had the nerve to then say, *Okay, I'm going to check this comedy thing out and apply myself the way I did with my engineering background*—which teaches you such discipline, which is what I always try to impart on young comedians starting, the discipline is really beyond comprehension. (CONTINUED)

Mr. Bob Golden

Stag Magazine

625 Madison Avenue

New York, N.Y.   Dec. 10, 1971

Dear Mr. Golden,

On September 10th I submitted two pages of jokes to you

for publication in Stag. Enclosed was a self-addressed

envelope, but I have not heard from your office in the

twelve weeks that have passed. If not interested in the

material which I sent you, please mail it back in the

self-addressed envelope enclosed with this letter.

Thank you.

                             Sincerely,

                             Garry Shandling

                             6638 Calle de San Alberto

                             Tucson, Arizona

                             85710

Garry sent his essays
and joke ideas out
for publication.
Left: A list of
magazine contacts.
Above: Following
up with a men's
magazine.

Garry Shandling
6638 Calle de San Alberto
Tucson, Arizona

(COPY)

MARIJUANA COMMERCIAL

INTRODUCTION: The way things are going, we may see the day when marijuana will be legalized, and although cigarette commercials have been banned on television, we really don't know whether marijuana commercials would be. I'd like to take you five years into the future and show you what you might be seeing on television between your favorite programs. I'd like you to use your imagination and make believe that this is a marijuana cigarette. Hmmm. Maybe you won't have to use your imagination.

Are you smoking more, but enjoying it less? Well then, come up, come <u>all</u> the way up to the taste of "Fly Aways." Have you been having bad trips? Then try "Fly Away" regulars, or "Fly Away" kings for extra mileage. We even have "Mary Jane Slims" for the ladies...or for you guys who aren't sure. "Mary Jane Slims;" the only marijuana cigarette with

Once I switched to the business college at the University of Arizona, I found it so easy that I had free time even in class. So I started to write monologues. I wanted to test myself, and I wrote a few George Carlin–type monologues around '70. Right when he was going through this new phase of what he was doing.

And I worked up the nerve to drive up to a club in Phoenix where he was playing. I'd never been in one of those clubs or anything. They didn't exist. There were no comedy clubs. And I managed to find him in the club, and asked him if he would read my material. He was really nice, and he said, "I write my own material." And I said, "I assumed." Which I did. And I said, "But there's nobody to give me feedback." (CONTINUED)

Marijuana Commercial   (2)

the new plastic removable tip. Or as we refer to it: the
plastic potholder.

My company, the R.B. Screwum Company, those fine
people who bring you "Happy Time LSD"...in an unbreakable
bottle, is proud to announce that a study done by fifty
qualified musicians has shown that our grass is greener!
And that's because the R.B. Screwum Company is located at
the place: mile high Denver.

So if you're tired of that old eight a.m. to five p.m.
rush, now it can always be twelve o'clock high. That's
right, when you smoke "Fly Aways" life is one big drag.
Don't be afraid to try "Fly Aways." Don't be chicken.
Our motto is: POT IN EVERY CHICKEN.

Now I don't want to fool you. You can get lung cancer
from "Fly Aways," but you won't care.

So look for "Fly Aways" on your grocer's shelf—it's
the pack with Whistler on the front—for you mothers out
there. On the back is the "Fly Away" bonus coupon. For
only twenty coupons you can get the best seller: "The
Alice B. Toklas I Hate to Cook Book."

Remember: You can take "Fly Aways" away from the fun,
but you can't take the fun away from "Fly Aways."

So Carlin said, "I'll read your stuff. Come back tomorrow night." I went back to the club the next night and he took me backstage and there was my material on his table. He said, "I looked at everything. You're very green, but I think you're funny. I think there's something funny on every page. And I think you should pursue it. If you're thinking of pursuing it, I think you should." And that's what gave me the kick to move to L.A. Because he was very sincere. And I was not the, as I say, the confident, arrogant type that thought, *Oh, man, I think I'm funny.*

I think he got an American Comedy Award, which is a thing that was happening about ten or twelve years ago, and they asked me to present it to him, because everybody knew that story, even though I hadn't really kept up with George. And I told that story. And he got up and the first thing he said is, to the audience, "I'm sorry . . . for encouraging Garry. It's my fault. I'm sorry." And he got such a big laugh.

Dear George,

This is the hardest thing I've had to write in the last five years, and you should know that includes a script for Three's Company.

I met you ten years ago at a club in Phoenix, Arizona called, "Mr. B's" -- a club obviously owned by a man who was not good with words. I was nineteen, in college to avoid the draft and in the process of deciding whether or not to pursue a career as a comedy writer -- a job that didn't qualify for an occupational deferment. You were standing by the bar and I asked you to read three pieces of material I had just written: a marijuana commercial, a routine about an anti-war march leader and one about a sex education class. I told you that you were the only comedian I would ever consider writing for and that feeling hasn't changed. I came to Los Angeles in 1972 and was fortunate to indeed begin a writing career, writing for Sanford & Son, Welcome Back Kotter, The Practice, The Harvey Korman Show and a couple of pilots. I'm sure you can remember when you were first starting in comedy how delicate the ego is at each small step. You reading my material was such an early step for me, and although it glared of my inexperience, your encouragement and kindness meant more at that time than I'm sure you realized. More so since you were a symbol in many ways of what I was striving for.

The recognition you truly deserve is still to come.
One day everyone will include your name among a list
of a handful of original comedic minds the likes of
Woody Allen, Mort Sahl, Richard Pryor and Lenny. I'm
still fighting a friend who's trying to get Corbett Monica
in there somewhere.

Since I first saw you in the mid-sixties -- before
your renaissance -- up until now, I have watched you
risk and watched you grow. I've seen the personal
conviction and the inner turmoil. Your humor has always
been an inspiration to me, but more importantly, the
kind of man you are has been an influence on me in my
own growth to be as funny as I can be, to know myself
and to be honest to myself and my fellow man. Whenever
I see you I'm reminded of these values.

Two years ago, at the peak of my writing career,
I called my agent and told him I no longer wanted to
write for television. It was time to listen to a voice
that was in me since I was ten years old. I wanted,
more than anything else, to be a comedian. I always did.
I'm still in the early stages of my development, working
out regularly at the Comedy Store and other clubs in town.
I've just begun doing some television; syndicated shows
like Make Me Laugh and The Comedy Shop. I've auditioned
for and will be doing "Merv" sometime in the next couple
of months. More important than these "career" steps is the

quality of work I'm trying to achieve, and this is always
first on my mind.

One of my goals is to one day meet you again. In
the meantime, I had to write and thank you for being
George Carlin. I hope you are well and that your new
paths lead to happiness and continued success.

Best,

Garry Shandling

GO WEST, YOUNG FUNNYMAN

In his early twenties, Garry set his sights beyond Tucson to the one place he could turn his comedic ambitions into reality: Los Angeles.

GARRY At the University of Arizona, I went to one year in graduate school, and then I moved here by myself because I thought, why bring my mother at that point. And you know, when I moved, my mother sued me for palimony. She said, "Twenty-two years you live with me and then move out just like that? I don't think so."

MIKE SHANDLING His father knew somebody, and they got him into the advertising agency—it was a Japanese agency—to write copy. So he was using writing skills. Of course, he's not writing his humor per se, and the first ad was a Suntory Whisky ad. It was a bottle of Suntory and a shot glass. It was sitting there and the tagline was "The shot heard 'round the world," and it was a big hit. And he was pretty proud of that, and we all thought that was pretty cool, because advertising is something. Our parents were printers. You weren't creative. You went to work and did your job and came home. So it was pretty cool.

ICE
CAPADES
LONG BEACH ARENA
APRIL 18 thru 22
APRIL 26 — MAY 13
LOS ANGELES
SPORTS ARENA

ADVENTURE IN MOVING

U-HAUL

7-10-75

7-10-75

RESUME:

~~Garry Shandling~~   Garry Shandling
~~6180 Canterbury Drive, #337~~   3914 1/2 Huron Ave.
~~Culver City, Calif. 90230~~   Culver City, Calif. 90230
~~TEL: 645-0573~~   TEL: 836-1399

PERSONAL DATA:

DATE OF BIRTH: November 29, 1949

PLACE OF BIRTH: Chicago, Ill.

MARITAL STATUS: Single

SOCIAL SECURITY:

EDUCATIONAL BACKROUND:

HIGH SCHOCL: Palo Verde High School, Tucson, Arizona.
Graduated 1967.

COLLEGE: Bachelor of Science degree in Marketing,
University of Arizona, 1971. Specialized
study in advertising. Also studied three
years of electrical engineering at University
of Arizona. Graduate work in creative
writing at UCLA and Universtiy of Arizona.

WORK EXPERIENCE:

1968-1969:   Employed by KUAT-TV, Tucson Arizona as
TV engineer. Also worked in production
and wrote TV news copy.

1970 TO PRESENT: Free-lance writer. Published several
short stories in magazines (e.g. People and
Places, and Valley). All are written in
the comedy style of Woody Allen and S.J.
Perelman. Also wrote comedy material for
comedians Louis Nye, Alan Bursky, George
Miller and Greg Shannon. Wrote material
for American Industrial Advertising awards
held in Los Angeles in February, 1974. Have
written several situation comedy scripts
which are currently in the hands of my agent.
(and where they will probably remain forever).

1973-1974:   Employed by Dentsu Advertising as copywriter.
Worked primarily on the

TEAC tape equipment account. Wrote print (both trade and consumer), radio, point-of-purchase, direct mail and collateral. Created basic slogan for '74 campaign: TEAC presents the creative world inside you.

Worked on Suntory whiskey account. Outdoor only.

Worked on Toyota industrial vehicles account. Trade, consumer print and collateral.

FEBRUARY 1974-MAY 1974: Employed by TN Productions to work on ABC's number one daytime television show The Girl in My Life. Researched and wrote new stories presented on the program.

Garry's mid-'70s résumé includes a gig working for *The Girl in My Life*, a one-season daytime series that was basically a distaff version of *This Is Your Life*.

GARRY It was culture shock: Here I was, a kid who had lived at home till he was twenty-two years old all through college, moved to Los Angeles, didn't know anybody, and insecure—not knowing whether this was going to be the right thing for me to do—and started hanging out at The Comedy Store, just watching. Never came to perform. And started writing scripts just to see if I could do it. I was a writer in high school, college I was a writer. I didn't have trouble getting words on paper. And I sat down one day and wrote an *All in the Family* script on spec and, just by some fluke, met somebody. I took a comedy writing class at UCLA and all you did was stand up and read your jokes, and I had to pay. I had to pay for that class to stand up and read jokes.

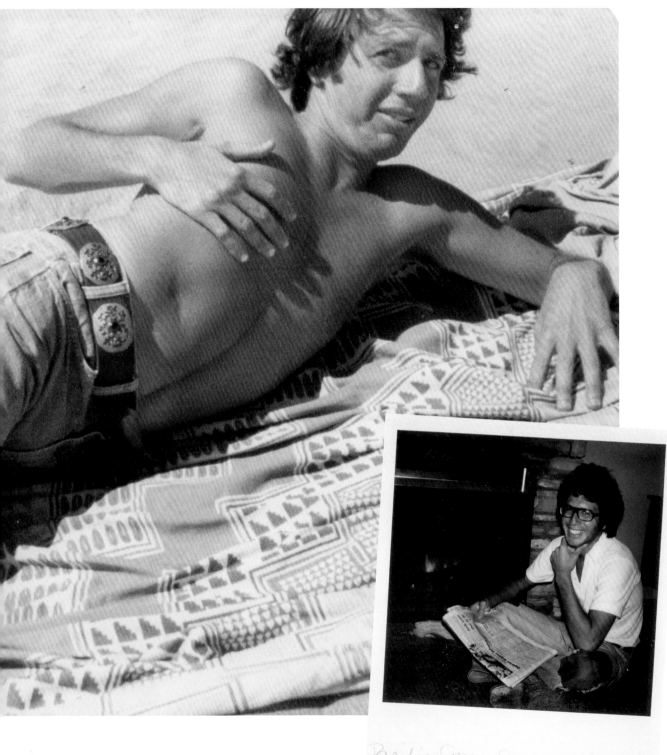

51

Pacific Grove Ca   9/23/75

The girl in Garry's life.

MIKE SHANDLING Wendy Vactor was his college girlfriend. She's from Tucson. She was very down-to-earth, very earthy. She came out to L.A. to go to school when Garry came—she was actually living here at that time. And they were boyfriend and girlfriend for probably five or six years. But I think once he got settled here, he realized he was just going in a different direction. Wendy was more of a down-to-earth normal, regular person, and probably wasn't gonna fit into that. We didn't really discuss that too much. He was pretty private. Relationships, especially at that time, he didn't really have too much to say. He would keep it to himself a little more.

Ping Pong is my life!

noon, Saturday

Dear Wendy,

Well, I just woke up, and I'm waiting for the sun to come out. I've been trying to sit in the sun whenever I have time, but so far this week the sun has come through the clouds only twice, and I was working then.

Yesterday was a very interesting day (Friday). To begin with, I spoke to the TEAC account executive at Dentsu (UA graduate), Bill Dubberly, and Larry Orinstein, the creative director, about my hours and so forth. It's amazing -- they are actually governing my work, but they didn't have the sleightest idea of what Gamo told me over the phone, or even what my salary was. So Dubberly kind of expected me to work 9 to 5. I told him that Gamo was hiring me on a more-or-less freelance basis and said that I could come in at ten o'clock or so, and leave in the afternoon. Then they asked me my salary, and I think they were surprised. So they agreed that I could come in around ten and then leave sometime in the afternoon -- when I want to. But they would like me in the office as much as possible so I can see what's going on. And I agree with that. (I figure on about 10:00 to 3:00)

I am at a disadvantage with Dentsu because they gave me my first job, so they feel they are just training me, although I know I can do ads as well as anybody. That's why when I go to a different agency after some experience, they'll view me in a different light -- not just as a kid to be trained who doesn't know his ass from the desk drawer.

To sum it all up; Dentsu is a very poorly organized agency, and unsophisticated for an American agency. And Gamo, well... I saw him wiping his desk drawer with toilet paper.

I left work about 3:30 yesterday; then came home and ate,
and then I went over to UCLA to look for a good game of Ping-Pong.
Well, it's unbelievable, but they don't have any tables in their
student union. There's bowlxing alleys, pool tables, and even
craft rooms, but no ping pong. One guy told me the tables were
in the dormitories, so off I went looking for the dorms. Each
dorm has a game room like the UA -- pinball machines, air hockey,
and a couple of ping-pong tables. But the ping-pong tables were
very poor and the lighting was awful, not nearly as good as the UA.
So I went to another dorm, and there were some guys playing pool,
and I asked about the ping-pong tables (I mean there has to be a
spot where all the good players meet). One of the guys put
down his cue, and said that he was the best in the dorm. Actually,
he seemed like a nice guy, so we played a few games on this dorms
crappy table. I haven't played in about 5 months, so I was quite
rusty. He won the first two games, then I won the next five in
a row. He quit, and was kind of nasty -- I guess he couldn't take
losing.

I played with him until 9:00 p.m.; then left and went over
to the Comedy Store, which is not too far away (just down Sunset.).
At the Comedy Store, I was taking with little Alan Bursky, He was
desperate to find someone to go with him to see "Enter the Dragon."
I'd already seen that (remember, I went with Greg), so when he got
up on stage to do his act, he told everyone he wanted to go to
the movies. After his act, two of his friends went with him.

Bursky led off his act with, "I was barmiztvahed by a very
reformed Rabi. A very reformed Rabbi. A Nazi." That's straight
form Woody Allen's album. I asked him about his obsession with

Woody Allen. He said he was working with Allen on an his new
movie, but when he went on the Tonite show, he had to quit.
He said Wooday Allen gave him some material to perform, and that
strangly enough, David Steinberg had used that same Nazi joke
on the Tonite show last week. We both agreed that was unbelievable,
although I didn't see all of David Steinberg when he was on,
particularly that joke.

I watched about 10 comedians, of which, George Miller was about
the third worst. His jokes are good, very good, he just has no
delivery, and his jokes don't fit his personality. He is a
real nice guy though, and we seem to get along well just talking.
He gave me a newspaper clipping about a greeting card company
that had come out with a sort of "insulting" line of cards, and
were making a fortune. One of the cards said, "In Oregon you
don't tan -- you rust." I don't know if you recall, but
I had written that joke for George about mixed parents, and that
when you're orange like me and go to the beach, you don't tan --
you rot." Quite a coincedence. (Woody Allen's line, I don't tan
-- I stroke, is by far the best of the three.)

Anyway, if it sounds like I'm such good friends with these
guys, I'm not. I just go there (I go in the back door now, so
they won't charge me),sit down in the back of the room and when
an occasion arises to chat with some of the performers or writers
I do. It's a very good way to meet people, and you never know
in the future when it might be beneficial that you would run
across someone you've talked to before.

I told George what I told you about my material. I consider
doing my own act every time I'm in the Comedy Store; if I could

just get the guts. When Alan Bursky flops -- which he does 90%
of the time-- I think about how I'd be sweating, and what a fool
I'd make of myself, although I realize that everybody has
sympathy for a flopping comedian, and really doesn't think any
less of him, except as a performer, not as a person.

When I'm not inthe comdey store, I'm my same lazy self,
and
xx that's what's so confusing. I really don't know what I want to
do.

Anyway, I hope you get this letter before we talk on the
phone, otherwise I have agreat tendency to repeat everything.
Everything is going well here, my cooking, the fish, the car,
and the laundry, but I miss you. I'm looking forward to
seeing youx just because you're you, for no other reason (would
you please bring patches, some food, a box of dish washing
detergent and a bottle of bleach).

I received a letter from Yumiko at Dentsu yesterday, uh-oh.

Take care, and I'll talk to you Monday.

Miss You,

Larry

P.S. Your letters are very funny — how would
you like to write some material?

I'm using a Cross pen — it's just not the same
as a Big Bar-ret now.

"Sanford & Rising Son"

GARRY There was a flood of young guys who came to L.A. As I called it, everybody who got in trouble in school flooded to L.A. to try and prove that what they were getting in trouble for could actually make them a living. The dream. And I got lucky quickly.

I think those were the days when they were looking for young writers, and somebody I literally bumped into first read a *M*A*S*H* script of mine—a writer, Ted Bergman, who really helped me. And he said, "This is your first spec script?" And I said, "Yeah." He said, "I think you're really talented," and he said, "I work on *Sanford and Son,* why don't you write a *Sanford and Son* spec script?" And I wrote one, sent it to him, he called me, he said, "It's not good enough, I can't submit it to the producers." And I asked him what was wrong with it and he actually gave me notes, and I rewrote it. All my friends said, "Don't rewrite it, they're never gonna read it again." And I rewrote it, and sent it to him, and he called me, he said, "This is the best outside"—meaning freelance —"spec script that we've ever gotten." And he sent it to the producers and I started writing *Sanford and Son,* of all things.

Annotated pages from the first of four teleplays Garry wrote for *Sanford and Son.*

<u>ACT ONE</u>

<u>FADE IN:</u>

<u>INT. LIVING ROOM - NIGHT</u>

(FRED IS SITTING IN HIS CHAIR, WATCHING TV AND SINGING ALONG)

FRED

    M-I-C. See you real soon.

    K-E-Y. Why? Because I'm stupid.

(LAMONT COMES IN FROM KITCHEN)

LAMONT

Hey Pop, come on. Dinner's ready.

(EXCITED)

FRED

HEY, SON, You don't know what you missed You missed Annette. She was...

~~I can't, Son. Annette's on next.~~

LAMONT

Come on! I've got a surprise in here.

(FRED RELUCTANTLY GETS UP AND TURNS TV OFF)

FR<u>E</u>D

Surprise? I hope you didn't burn dinner

again. Black may be beautiful, but not when

it's on my meatloaf.

(THEY BOTH WALK INTO THE KITCHEN. AH CHEW'S BACK IS TO THEM AS HE STIRS A BIG POT ON THE STOVE.)

FRED

Okay, what's the surprise?

(AH CHEW TURNS AROUND. HE'S WEARING A HIGH CHEFS CAP THAT HAS WRITTEN ON THE RIM: JAPANESE POWER.)

AH CHEW

Hi, Mr. Sanford.

59

                    FRED

You're smarter than I thought, Ah Chew.

                LAMONT

(ANGERLY)

                                want to start
    Okay, that's it! If you ~~want~~ fooling

around with this restaurant -- go ahead!

But you're not going to have anything to do

with the ~~Dad~~ junk business. I'll handle it

alone. Just stay out of my way.

                    FRED

That's fine with me. You run the junk

business and I'll run the take-out restaurant.

But when I make my first million, and you're

                            asking for the keys
broke, don't comearound ~~expecting to get~~

to my Lincoln Continental.

~~a discount on egg roll.~~

CUT TO:

LIVING ROOM
INT. ~~KITCHEN~~ - DAY
(NERVOOS ABOUT THEIR FIRST DAY) → SITTING BY THE
                                    TELEPHONE)
                AH CHEW

Did you put the ad in the paper, Mr.

Sanford?

                    FRED
        the telephone should start ringing anytime
Yeah, ~~xxxxxxxxxxxxxxxxxxxxxxxxxxxxxxxxxxxx~~
now.
~~xxxxxxxxxx~~

(KNOCK AT THE DOOR) ~~xxxxxxxxxxx~~ GRABS THE PHONE)
(AH CHEW ~~xxxxxxxxxxxxxxx~~

            AH CHEW
Hello? Hello?
~~boy, you sure have a sick sounding telephone.~~

(FRED GIVES AH CHEW A LOOK. GOES TO ANSWER THE DOOR.)
~~(IT'S GRADY.)~~
            FRED
It's the door, dummy. Go into the kitchen
and get things ready.

GARRY Across the hallway was *Welcome Back, Kotter*. And so I walked up to the front desk and said, "Hi, is there a story editor around? I'm writing for *Sanford and Son*." And she said, "Let me get him." And this guy came out and I said, "Listen, I'm writing some scripts for *Sanford and Son*, and I wrote a spec for *Welcome Back*." So they called me and they said, "We want you to write a spec script for us."

ERIC COHEN (head writer, *Welcome Back, Kotter*) I was pretty much the head writer and producer of the show at that point. I remember the episode. It was a good show, "Horshack vs. Carvelli."

JUDD It is funny that he wrote the Horshack show.

ERIC COHEN Well, you know, this is the advice that you learn. You want to break in, don't write the character that everyone is writing. My guess is, that's how Garry sold that episode, because everybody came in with Travolta episodes.

WELCOME BACK, KOTTER

"Horshack vs. Carvelli"

#214

20-WBK-76

Written by

Garry Shandling

Produced by

George Yanok

and

Eric Cohen

Executive Script Consultants

Jerry   Jewel Jaffee
              and
Rannow   Rannow

THE KOMACK COMPANY, INC.

in association with

Wolper Productions

4151 Prospect Avenue

Hollywood, California 90027

FINAL DRAFT

November 20, 1976

                    BARBARINO

For what?

                    CARVELLI

For the boxing match between your

school and mine.

                    BARBARINO

Where?

                    CARVELLI

The "Silver Gloves" boxing championship, next

week. I finally get to prove in front

of everyone who's the best fighter.

                    BARBARINO

Yeah? Well any one of my guys can take

any one of your guys!

                    CARVELLI

Where, to a dance?

(CARVELLI'S GUYS CRACK UP)

                    HORSHACK

Hey Carvelli! Your face is so ugly,they

close it down on weekends so little kids

won't see it.

(ARNOLD LAUGHS. CARVELLI CAN'T STAND THE LAUGH AND
COVERS HIS EARS)

                    CARVELLI

Can't something be done medically for

this punk?

(HE THINKS FOR A SPLIT SECOND, THEN TO BARBARINO:)

Okay Pretty Boy, I accept your challenge!

Garry's sole episode of *Welcome Back, Kotter,* "Horshack vs. Carvelli."

Is it because I can't stand situation comedy or can't I do it? Or is it a combination. I must say I dislike it but I dislike my ability not to be able to write it well. Where will this lead? I am going to see Jw in 2 days — I am totally confused and having difficulty writing. And yet I still am funny verbally.

Hal intimidates one with his mind. Robin intimidates me with his humor. I am questioning everything about myself from my intelligence to my humor, Why?
Why do compare myself to others?
— I am horney.

1977

GARRY I was at a story meeting for *Three's Company*. I'd written a first draft and one of the producers looked at a line in the script and said, "Well, Chrissy wouldn't say that." And it was like a voice from God. I thought, *I don't think I can do this for the rest of my life*. I stopped right then and went on to perform.

JOHN MARKUS (writer, *The Larry Sanders Show*) He had made a vow that he was going to sell his van before he went back to it. He would run out of all his money before he would return to writing for sitcoms. And he wrote for some good shows. I mean he wrote for *The Harvey Korman Show,* which was a good show. He spent a season on that and wrote some episodes. His only staff job, and he had all the scripts laying around his house, and he just realized that it would not make use of what he could do in life.

GARRY I went to a shrink, because I was sitting at a typewriter one day and I froze. Just like when I was in engineering in college and I said I don't know if I wanna do this my whole life. I said I think I wanna try this stand-up thing because—and here's the key to my comedy—I think it'll allow me to discover something about myself. I hadn't grown up yet, I didn't know myself. And I thought, *If I sit here, I'm never gonna discover it*. I remember how scared I was. I never was driven to perform for the love of the audience, for money, for ego of doing my own material, none of that. I needed to tune in to who I was, and I thought this might be an interesting avenue.

GARRY I would go to The Comedy Store and I would watch. I'd just sit in the back and watch. And I thought, *Who has the nerve to do that?* And I challenged myself to go up on an amateur night one time. And God played this great trick on me: I got some laughs the first time I went onstage. And I walked off that stage and I thought, *My God, this could be a way I could find out who I am.*

GARRY (from his first-ever Comedy Store set)
You don't know what it was like being an unwanted child. My mother had tried to talk her doctor into performing an abortion, but he said he wouldn't do it because it was illegal to perform an abortion once the child had reached the age of fifteen.

Notes on improving the act.

THINGS TO IMPROVE ACT: Smoother, more flowing -- every joke and thought flows into another--, tighter, TIGHTER, TIGHTER, Work moment to meomnet-- every moment is a gem --, consistent energy -- don't back off, get them and hold them, kFunnier matbrial, still funnier material. TIGHTER! FLOW! MOMENT TO MOMENT!! The performer must give of himself and the more open, the more liked--regardless of material (Dick Shawn is brilliian but does not give of himself. David Brenner is good despite his materia̋l because he enjoys every moment, and is himself. He sells the material!) Flow vocally. Pack and tighten! Kick ass.

This is my first time at the COMEDY STORE, so I

thought I'd just spend the next few minutes telling

you a little about myself. I was born in Chicago, Illinois.

Then when I was two years old my parents moved to

Arizona. I wish they would have told me. You don't
It's true, my parents beat me.
parents were not fond of me.
know what it's like coming home to an empty house. My

parents to put it lightly, were just onnot fond off me,

I think they somehe-- It was right after I was born that

my mother began taking birth control pills. I was forced

to swim at a very young age. When °I was one and-a-hal
slow reader
year old my father threw me in a wishing well for "Gone With

good luck. But I finally made it to Arizona and it was the Wind.

in Arizona that I cheated and scratched my way through

elementary school, Junior high and high school and
finally graduated from the U of A.
college. but It was in high school that I met my first
Both
unforgettable character: My P.E. teacher, Mr. Blitz.

If you all recall, PE.E teachers are not bright, right?
He went to college on a pinball scholarship. (FLASHCARDS)
ANd Mr. Blitz fit into that caaegory with room to spare.

I remember one of the more tragic exeperiences in high

school. One day our principal snuck into the gymnasium

and committed suicide by hanging himself on the fings.

The next day Mr. Blitz, our P.E. insturctor, walked in,

saw him hanging there......gave him a 9.8. Mr. Blitz

had spent five years constructing a giant sundial in his

yard. Then he got a hernia trying to wind it. And what

of my lack of fulfillment
over things that "should"
make me happy ~~and~~
exists because what I
am doing is not what I
want - so how can it be
fulfilling. Therefore,
instead of getting upset
~~o~~ over not being happy
at something I "should"
happy about, I should
look at it see what
needs to be changed
because there is no
"should" for me —

I am me, ~~Before~~ I'VE
ALREADY PROVED
THAT THE "SHOULDS"
DON'T WORK FOR
ME!! " SO WHY
LIVE BY THEM
ANY LONGER?

Shoulds:	Happiness?
1) Electrical engineering	NO
2) Ad agency	NO
3) Girl in my life	NO
4) Living with Wendy	NO
5) Sanford & SMS	NO
6) Staff job	NO

1977

FROM NEARLY DYING TO KILLING: GARRY BECOMES A STAND-UP

On September 10, 1976, Garry was at the intersection of Wilshire and Santa Monica in Beverly Hills when a speeding car nearly ended his career before it ever began. He survived the accident with a changed outlook, the brush with death cementing his ambition at last: to master the art of stand-up comedy.

I'm not afraid of death, its living that scares the hell out of me — you can get killed out there.

GARRY I had a car accident when I was twenty-seven in which I was nearly killed. I had a vivid near-death experience that involved a voice asking, "Do you want to continue leading Garry Shandling's life?" Without thinking, I said, "Yes." Since then, I've been stuck living in the physical world while knowing, without a doubt, that there's something much more meaningful within it all. That realization is what drives my life and work.

You've grown as a man and had many personal relationships.

Remember when you were hit by the car? Death was in your face and you realized, just to live — even with nothing is a more than fair trade. What do you need? NOTHING. If you had everything, you would still have to face death.

Don't be attached to life. Let go of everything. See what's left.

Aug. 15

I'm kapa kua. Enjoyed 4 seasons on Big island a bit more. Different here now. Maybe I'll go home early.

1998

73

or my Ernie? Is a script more important than living? Dieing people lose their materialism. That's because they see the truth. I saw the truth after my accident. I've just forgotten about it. I won't do this any more. The truth is is that if youre dieing youll give $100,000 to live - even in a shack. So how important is money compared to one's life - NOTHING.

1977

From Nearly Dying to Killing: Garry Becomes a Stand-up

GARRY As they strapped the oxygen mask to my face, I lifted it up and said, "Don't trim my hair too short in the back." It's a cliché, but there's a very thin line between comedy and tragedy. I know that line in my professional life. I'm not so sure I know it in my personal life.

...but because I love the laugh chemistry. I will commit myself to becoming a stand up comic - totally. I will not look back. I will not "fall back" on my writing. I will not consider what will happen if I don't make it, because once I commit myself it is done!

When I do stand up, each time, I work, I will feel the thrill of getting laughs —

GARRY The accident gave me some actual insight into life and its impermanence. That there is something else to it than what meets the eye. That was my actual experience. And so I realized I'd best try to figure out who I authentically was. And I could do that through stand-up. And I just said to my writing agent: "I can't do this." And he said, "Well, do you think you can make it as a comic?" I said, "I don't know, but if I don't try now I won't know." That's what attracted me to stand-up: *I can't do this because for some reason I don't quite know who I am, and I have to find out.*

WELCOME TO THE COMEDY STORE...

Like folk music in Greenwich Village or cabaret in Weimar Berlin, stand-up comedy found its epicenter on the Sunset Strip in the '70s and '80s—and Garry was there for all of it. Over the course of four years, he would go from begging for spots at The Comedy Store, stand-up's cathedral in L.A., to debuting the closely honed set on *The Tonight Show* that launched his career into its next phase. But first he had to get through Mitzi.

Pauly Shore   Arsenio Hall   Eddie Murphy   Tamayo's

George Carlin   Joey Lawan   Bob Goldthwait   Louise Ouart

Mike Binder   Whoopi Goldberg   Barry Sobel   Louie Anderson

Robie Diamond   Argus Hamilton   Damon Wayans

Cybebun Burr   Bud Cort

the
Mainroom

MAIN ROOM
& CO.
ARGUS HAMILTON
VALERY PAPPAS
TAMAO OTSUKA
WILLY TYLER & LE
JAMES STEPHENS
T. 30

A. REEV
HAV
WILLY PAF
OR BEHR

I like to think when I play a club, while I don't always entertain the audience, they certainly feel better leaving, because they're not me.

BOB SAGET (comedian) It was rumbling. It was rock and roll. Steve Martin had already gone off and changed the world with twenty thousand people at a concert. Letterman was one of my first hosts. Billy Crystal would go up, he was on *Soap*. He watched me do my stand-up with my guitar. I'd sit at the back of the room and Billy would tell me how funny I was and then tell me, "Just try to get on a good show that you like," and he just, like, befriended me. And then I met Garry, because we had similar time spots and I was hosting, and it was just a huge amount of energy. I mean, it was crazy. And Robin Williams would go up, and Jeff Altman and Michael Keaton. Michael Keaton had the best bit, which was when his arms would fall asleep. I became a regular, and I started hosting a lot at the Westwood Store. Michael Richards would play with his little toy figures. I mean, comedy was so popular in '78, '80, '81, it was rock and roll.

GARRY I used to come on amateur nights, so it's one night a week. And eventually, that was even cut for me to you'd come every other week on amateur night, which meant you'd not necessarily even get on. You'd come at seven o'clock, sign in, and on some nights I didn't even get on, which meant I sat here from seven at night till two in the morning, waiting to see if my name was going to be called. That's how it worked.

> WOMEN
> I just broke up with my girl friend. She moved in with another guy. I figured, that's as good a reason as any to break-up.

Sept. 7

How to write everything I feel?

Saw *Jaw*, and learned that I must trust my instincts. This is a turning point in my life. I had Norman tell 3's Company I'm not doing a second draft. I couldn't believe how understanding Paul Wayne was. Now I am just about ready to quit the Harvey Korman Show. I am going to pursue the top - stand-up.

I have the same feeling as when I dropped engineering in college, quit Dentsu, quit girl in my life and now finally Harvey Korman. I am worried about disappointing Hal - I love him and I hope we can remain good friends. I am ready to immerse myself in obtaining my goal of achieving the best stand-up performance I can - that is all I can do - the best I can. When I master being myself on stage, I will be a star - I know this. God, for the first time I see it. I KNOW WHAT I MUST DO AND I WILL DO IT. NOTHING EVER FELT SO RIGHT!

LEWIS SMITH (friend/actor) I was there when Mitzi Shore walked up to him and said, "Garry, I wish you wouldn't come on Monday nights. You're not even as good as the amateurs. You're never gonna make it, Garry. You're not funny." He was devastated. And I was pissed off. We were driving home in the car because I'm out of work too. I said, "You can't let someone talk to you that way," but she was the queen of comedy. For a comedian to have someone like that say that to you, it's like God talking to you in a way. And his ability to transcend that and not quit was pretty amazing. She meant it. That was not like a coaching session. It would've been nice if it was. She meant it. She thought she was helping him.

MERRILL MARKOE (writer) Garry had the same problem with Mitzi that I did. Mitzi had a very firm opinion that you could not be a writer and a performer. She felt those were two entirely different areas, and if she knew that you had taken work as a writer, you were out. That was the problem Garry was having with her. And so was I. I might have been more stoppable than Garry, but she wouldn't book you if she thought you were a writer. She felt that was a betrayal of stand-up. It was an old-fashioned opinion of writing and performing. I think it was

> Oct. 10
> Just got back from not working at the Comedy Store — it was like the old days, being bumped by one of Mitzi's showcases. But what wasn't like the old days is my attitude and growth is so obvious that I am very happy — I feel I am going to go through many "tests" in my ordeal to make it. Each test will make me stronger.
> I still know that what I have above all the other comics is my likeability — and specialness.

1977

left over from vaudeville, where a comedian had his writers. And you weren't both. It hurt him. She wouldn't go past that, she didn't like that. She thought that meant that you weren't committed enough.

It will just take the right person to see it. I have been so secure in this likeability that I have forgotten to some extent that I must find the material that works for ME. I am concentrating on my acting. I've been on stage so few times in my life— it's just going to take time. I now see a somewhat different plan, I must speed up

JAY LENO (late-night host) Mitzi ruled with an iron hand. I felt sorry for people. There was a very funny comedian named Jack Graham. And, well, she thought he should be "Jackie Banana" and wear a yellow jacket. So he became Jackie Banana to work at The Comedy Store. And there were people who didn't really appreciate the notes. And if you'd worked the Improv— I managed to do both, I was one of the few that was lucky enough, but I knew people that go, "Oh, you worked the Improv. You can't work here." So you were forced to take sides. But, overall, it was a great place to work. It was fun. I don't know what other problems Mitzi had. I don't know whether she was an expert on comedy or not. It was just her opinion, and she owned the baseball field, so you played by those rules.

Garry and Mitzi Shore, owner and gatekeeper of The Comedy Store.

Garry and Lewis Smith.

Bye

Thursday

Dear Mom and Dad,

Suprise! I'm the last person you expected to get a letter from.

I've received all your checks. You know that if you weren't helping me, I couldn't be doing the things that I'm doing -- that is, to constantly keep my mind on my writing. But I really would like to get some work. Perhaps the "wishing well" commercial well come through with that agency. They really like it, and I'm sure it can bring them a new account...which does me a lot of good (except that I might finally be able to put a TV commercial in my portfolio which will be a great help).

I was pretty down after going to the Comedy Store Monday night. Mitzy is an asshole (You know I ususally don't speak that way, so you can imagine what I think of her.). Anyway, I do have some good news for a change, although, as I keep telling you, you don't know anything until something finally happens, but I did get some great encouragement last night in my comedy workshop.

As I told you, Jack DeLeon is the director for comedy of Tony Orlando and is on "Barney Miller." He also does stand-up comedy (I've never seen him), and says he's doing Las Vegas this summer with Dionne Warwick. *or Tony Orlando* Well, anyway, towards the end of class (This is a class of several experienced actors -- the average age is close to 40, and there are people who have been on TV and have done

plays on Broadway.) so, as I was saying, towards the end
of class, there was a girl who had written a stand-up
routine and wanted to try it. She was far below average
i n both delivery, *and material* although not as bad as some at
the Comedy Store (who get better times than me). She went
over with mixed reaction -- I laughed once and smiled
three times.

Don't ask me where I got the courage ~~from~~, but I
said I would like to do *my monolog* ~~also~~. It was difficult for me
to do it, especially since Monday night had left me
very depressed. I did my normal eight or nine minutes.
The reaction was just short of sensational, particularly
since there were only about sixteen people. Everyone
laughed at everything. Jack DeLeone was cracking up, and
afterward we had an open session where everyone gave
me their comments (our class is based on total honesty,
so they weren't afraid to give criticism), and it was
all favorable, with a few minor suggestions. Jack DeLeone
also asked me if I would write for him for his Las Vegas
show, and he wants to look at my scripts and sketches.
I told everyone the trouble I was having *with* Mitzy, and there
was a unanamous chorus of "screw her!". Many people knew
her, some personally, and said she is a total whacko.
Jack DeLeone said he would help me get into some other
clubs. He thinks I have a long way to go as a stand-up
comedian (which I feel also), but said I have a fantastic
comedic mind. He told the class that if Shecky Green had

my level of humor, he would be a superstar.

Needless to say, this encouragement was worth all
the money in the world. And if nothing develops out of
his help (which it may not), the encouragement and
exposure were worth it. The Comedy Store and Mitzy can
get you extremely depressed, and she can be very
degrading. Of course, I try and roll with the punches,
but sometimes it is very difficult. I know that if I
stay in this business I am in for even worse times, and
this is something I have to decide for myself -- is it
all worth it? I don't know yet. I hope I'll be able
to firmly make a decision soon as to just how dedicated
I'm going to become. I have such a long way to go.

In any case, I want you to know that I'm looking
forward to coming into Tucson. I know that getting
away for awhile will do me good, but I must finish the
projects I have going before I come in. I don't see
any problems, but sometimes something comes up at the last
minute. Jack DeLeone was already asking me how long I'd
be gone, because he wants to get started with the
writing. It is really an amazing transistion: he talked
to me at the first two classes as teacher to student, but
after he heard my monolog he was asking for my help.
I also have to complete a Carol Burnette sketch I'm writing
before I leave.

Anyhow, I wanted to drop you a line with some
good news for a change. A lot of times I don't write
because the letters would sound so negative. So tonight
I feel more encouraged and confident again, and that

will keep me going for awhile. As with all the other
comedians, insecurity is a prime factor -- and rejection
or approval can make all the difference in the world.

I think this is the longest letter I've ever written
without being funny, so I'll just give you a joke:

I have bad luck with pets. I had a beautiful
Irish Setter that I had adopted from the Humane
Society. When he was eight years old, I told
him I had adopted him, and he ran away to look
for his real parents.

If you didn't laugh, never mind. If you did laugh, please
t ape it and send it to Mitzy in care of the Comedy Store.

I'm looking forward to seeing you all. Get the
golf clubs ready.

Love,

[signature]

MERRILL MARKOE Monday night at The Comedy Store, and there was Garry with his jar of Ovaltine. Because he's a man on the town carrying a jar of Ovaltine everywhere. And then there were a number of other memorable places that he and I made jokes about for the whole rest of the years that I knew him. For instance, there was a disco in Reseda, on a Thursday night—it was like a sort of an unpopular disco because if you were gonna go to a disco, why go to Reseda? It had a comedy break in the middle and there was half a roomful of people dancing and then they'd shut everything down, and stand-ups would have to go into the center of the disco and do a few minutes. It was pretty deadly. Everybody worked for free at all of those things. The Comedy Store pre-strike was entirely free.

The other place that I ran into him that made both of us laugh for the entire rest of his life was a vegetarian restaurant on Melrose Avenue called the Natural Fudge Café. He was always for the whole rest of his life saying to me, "So you doing any spots at the Natural Fudge Café?" And that place—talk about deadly. It was eerie—your act was greeted with an eerie silence that was only broken by the faint scraping of utensils breaking veggie burgers. And then no other sounds.

1979

Dealing with heckler:
Relate) retort to audience, not to heckler. Continue flow talking about heckler (not spending 5 mins talking to heckler and thus alienating the rest of audience. Tie heckler into existing material. Tie heckler retort into material you're speaking about and maintain flow.

From Nearly Dying to Killing: Garry Becomes a Stand-up

Keep the mind pure,
To do all that is good,
Not to commit evil.

Patience.

~~fear~~

Dec 30.

Becomes clearer
each day that
hanging around

1979

GARRY It was really hard, stand-up's really hard, and you have to go through enormous rejection. When a crowd just doesn't go for it, and they're heckling at the same time, and you're not at that stage yet to handle it, I remember days just sitting in my car driving back from the club and not getting out of the car for a half hour after I drove into the driveway. But I would do the late shows in Cleveland, and so people would say, "Now, how come you seem so comfortable on *The Tonight Show*?" You go, "Oh, this is nothing!"

Comedy store is not
healthy in way of success or
as a person. It will
seem silly to read all
this space devoted to the
Comedy store when I look
back on this journal. It
is like high school.

WHEN A JOKE BOBMS: Maybe that joke was off key. (TAKE OUT PITC
TONE HORN AND PLAY DIFFERENY PITECHES AN D REPEAT PUNCH
LINE AT DIFFERENT PITCHES.

Eddie Landers was one
of Garry's earliest alter
egos. A melvin of the
highest order, complete
with shirtfront pulled
through his fly, Landers let
Garry hone his comedy
of self-deprecation.

MERRILL MARKOE Before he started doing it in his act—that whole thing about "How's my hair, how's my hair?"—he did use to obsessively do that all the time. He said that almost every time I ever saw him. That was not a bit. But he was self-aware enough to make it into a bit, and that was part of his charm. He was very self-aware.

GARRY I used to purely think that my appearance was all based on my hair and how it came out that day, but not really. But I went out onstage one day and said, "How's my hair today?" When I kind of noticed that I was concerned how my hair looked, I was able to objectively say, "Wow—that's a little neurotic attitude." And I explored that onstage and it became part of the act. It was all based on something real and then exaggerated for humor. But tell me, how do you think my hair looks today?

Sept 18 & 19 & 20 — 1977

Camping for the second day — now at Big Sur.

Some important thoughts:

1) Stage freight is caused by not living in the now — it is caused by living in the future: "Will I play my roll well? Will I be liked? What will I say?"

Yet if I just get up and do whatever Garry Shandling would do, there is no reason to be anxious — because

Whatever I do will
be Harry Shandling, and
that is who I am.
I am who I am.
There is no reason to
be afraid of what people
think, because I am
being me — all I have
is me — what I do —
who I am is all I
have. I do what I
do. WHAT THE
HELL DIFFERENCE DOES
IT MAKE WHAT THEY
THINK. WHAT I THINK
AND AM IS MY CENTER

I saw Jeff Altman KILL!
Kill like I never have.
this is not a comparison —
there was something to learn:
use everything you've got
to be funny, I can still
see more of myself: more
voices, more faces, more
character, more attitude,
more presence, more
energy, more sounds,
more broad material, more
crazy material.
But to work clubs
across the country—the

1979

I am growing.

May 30

Listening to Elvis today on the radio, I realized he can sing <u>any</u> song and it is still Elvis. The Material doesn't matter. To Elvis. People don't think, "oh, he's singing that song — Perry Como sings that." No one cares. No one realizes. They want to hear Elvis. So it is with Material. It doesn't matter if it's like someone else. It is merely a vehicle to be funny. The more you are funny and the less you worry about the song you are singing, the more you'll be yourself. The

1979

ED SOLOMON (writer, *It's Garry Shandling's Show*) I think for Garry, for his whole life, it was about finding himself. Like the search for himself. And I think, when he was trying to figure out who he was as a comedian, he was trying to figure out himself. He was always trying to find, *Where am I, truthfully, in this? And how can I be not just doing jokes and jokes?* Because at first he was just doing jokes. He was doing *Make Me Laugh,* the show, and he was doing stuff with Ovaltine, and he'd take a drink of powdered Ovaltine, get the chocolate in his mouth, and he was doing joke after joke, but he was never happy about that. He was always saying, *What's true here? What's true here? Who am I in this? Where am I?* And you know, Garry in life, and in his act, would circle around things. And circle around things. And circle around things. He didn't care how funny— I mean, he obviously wanted to be really funny. But the idea for him wasn't to just kill in the room. It was to get closer to some idea that he had about himself.

JAY LENO I first met Garry when the comedy strike was going on. He'd just come to Los Angeles, and in that bemused "I want to be a comedian . . ." way. It was this comedy strike was going on, they were trying to get twenty-five dollars a set for comedians, because the clubs were booming, making a fortune, you couldn't even get free food or anything. So everybody was on strike, and he was like, "How'd I get stuck in the middle of this? I can't go on? I just got here." You know when he gets that "Huh?"—that confused look on his face. I always remember just laughing at his predicament. I go, "It's not that big a deal, it'll be all right." He just had that way about him.

DAVE COULIER (comedian) Garry was a writer, primarily, so he was getting late-night spots. He would get like the 12:15 slot in the original room at The Comedy Store. It took a while, but he crafted his jokes so well that every night you'd see it start to take on a funnier shape, and you just knew, *Okay, this guy is an amazing joke writer*. And then I think his performance level caught up to his ability to write the jokes.

DRUGS

I used to use drugs ~~because~~ but I had to stop because I'm Jewish, and as a Jew you can only feel good for so long.

FUNNY OR NOT
FUNNY!! FUCK IT!
WHO CARES?!
I'm tered so tired.
of wondering. I am
ready to give myself
up. I can't take
it any more. I don't
want to think about
what I'm doing. I
don't want to worry or
pressure myself. I
CAN'T THINK OF

BEING GOOD ENOUGH
ANY LONGER.

GOD HELP ME
PLEASE! I give
myself up to you.
I can't! Please—
I just want to enjoy
my life. I don't
want it ruled by my
work!
      I must clear
my head and never
think about this SHIT.

I'm so Fucking tired
depressed. TIRED OF
WORRYING. I CAN
GIVE IT ALL UP
OR JUST STOP
WORRYING AND SEE
WHAT HAPPENS.
FUCK ABOUT WORRYING
I DON'T CARE WHAT
HAPPENS ANYMORE,
I'd rather not be
a success than to go
through this.
These cycles I go through

are a pain in the ass.
I'm just going let myself
feel like shit now, then
FUCK IT ALL
          These biorhythm
cycles or whatever they
are. FUCK IT. LEAVE.
ME ALONE. MY MIND
LEAVE ME ALONE.
I HATE IT. I
CAN'T WORRY ANYMORE
DO YOU UNDERSTAND!?
I'M TIRED OF DESIRES —
GOALS. LEAVE ME THE
FUCK ALONE. FUCK OFF!!

I DON'T EVEN WANT TO BE A GREAT COMEDIAN ANY MORE. I JUST WANT TO HAVE FUN AND BE HAPPY. THIS IS NATURAL AND COMES FROM GOD AND YOU ARE GOD. ONLY YOU'RE FUCKING MIND INTERRUPTS. KEEP IT STILL ASSHOLE! I'M FUCKING TIRED. GET THE FUCK OFF MY BACK GARRY. GO DUMP YOUR MIND IN THE TOILET. YOU GO ON TV WHEN YOU WANT TO, NOT WHEN THEY WANT YOU.

YOU CONTROL YOUR LIFE, NO ONE ELSE, ONLY YOU CAN EXERT PRESSURE ON YOURSELF.

NO STRIVING, NO GOALS. ITS OVER THIS HAS TO BE IT. I CAN'T TAKE IT ANYMORE

You do what you want. stand for what you feel and believe. Don't allow anyone to judge you or tell you

READY FOR PRIME TIME

For comedians of the era, no grail was holier than that of clinching a spot on *The Tonight Show with Johnny Carson*—except for maybe getting called over to the couch by Johnny. Garry was no exception, and on March 18, 1981, he distilled everything he had learned about comedy into a rock-solid six-minute set, turning in a star-making debut on the biggest show in America.

GARRY I had just signed with the William Morris Agency and they brought Jim McCawley to see me. I did so well the night he came to see me that he said, "You were so good. I have to come back tomorrow night to see it again to see if it wasn't a fluke." And he came back the next night and it went well again, and he booked me. The next week I was on *The Tonight Show*. And really a great first appearance on *The Tonight Show*.

Garry fulfilled his dream of performing on *The Tonight Show with Johnny Carson*. He would fulfill it many more times, as guest and as host, in the coming years.

JOHNNY CARSON (speaking to audience after Garry's set) It's nice to see somebody new come out and really have some funny material. His name is Garry Shandling. You'll hear a lot about him.

JOHN MARKUS My biggest memory comes from when he first appeared on *The Tonight Show,* because I was there, I was standing just outside the greenroom and watching it on television and there was about six or seven of us there, and first of all I remember him killing. And I remember when he came offstage he collapsed. This was so overpowering—not just the reaction from the audience but the fact that he got to the top of the mountain at that point, and I think he had to spend every ounce of what he had to get there and to pull it off that he collapsed. We were around him, so we held on to him and he cried. So my memory of it is the emotion.

I think there was a part of him that wondered if the cost was, like, worth it. He didn't specifically say that, but he would talk about how he had nothing left. That he gave it all, and *Is it okay? Did I do all right?* And he approached it from a place of *How empty am I?* Garry felt like he had finished a journey, and in a way, he was right. I think his whole methodology was to basically fall over the finish line for something.

JAY LENO It used to be, if you're on *Ed Sullivan,* everybody in America saw you. For Johnny Carson it was the same thing. When Johnny had *The Tonight Show,* if anybody had their TV on at 11:30, that's what they watched. If you were on *The Tonight Show,* the next day, "Hey, hey, I saw you, hey, were you that guy?" That was the difference between being a professional and not being a professional. If you did *The Tonight Show,* agents would take your call, people would listen to you. "Did he sit down?" "Yeah, he sat down, Johnny invited him over, first set." If they didn't see it then they want to get the kinescope, or they want to get the tape of it.

BABIES

My friend has an 18 month old baby. And parents think everything their baby does is cute. The kid loaded his diaper — good old number 2, right. The wife says, "Shannon made a gift for Daddy." Now this guy must be awfully easy to shop for on Father's Day.

My sheepdog kicks when he sleeps. My friend says, "That means your dog's having a nightmare." Now, what's a nightmare for a dog? Did you ever stop to think about it? He's drinking out of the toilet and the lid falls?

The vet gave me these animal tranquilizers to give my dog. They're doggy downers or something. I don't know whay they are, but they tasted real minty and they're hard to swallow.

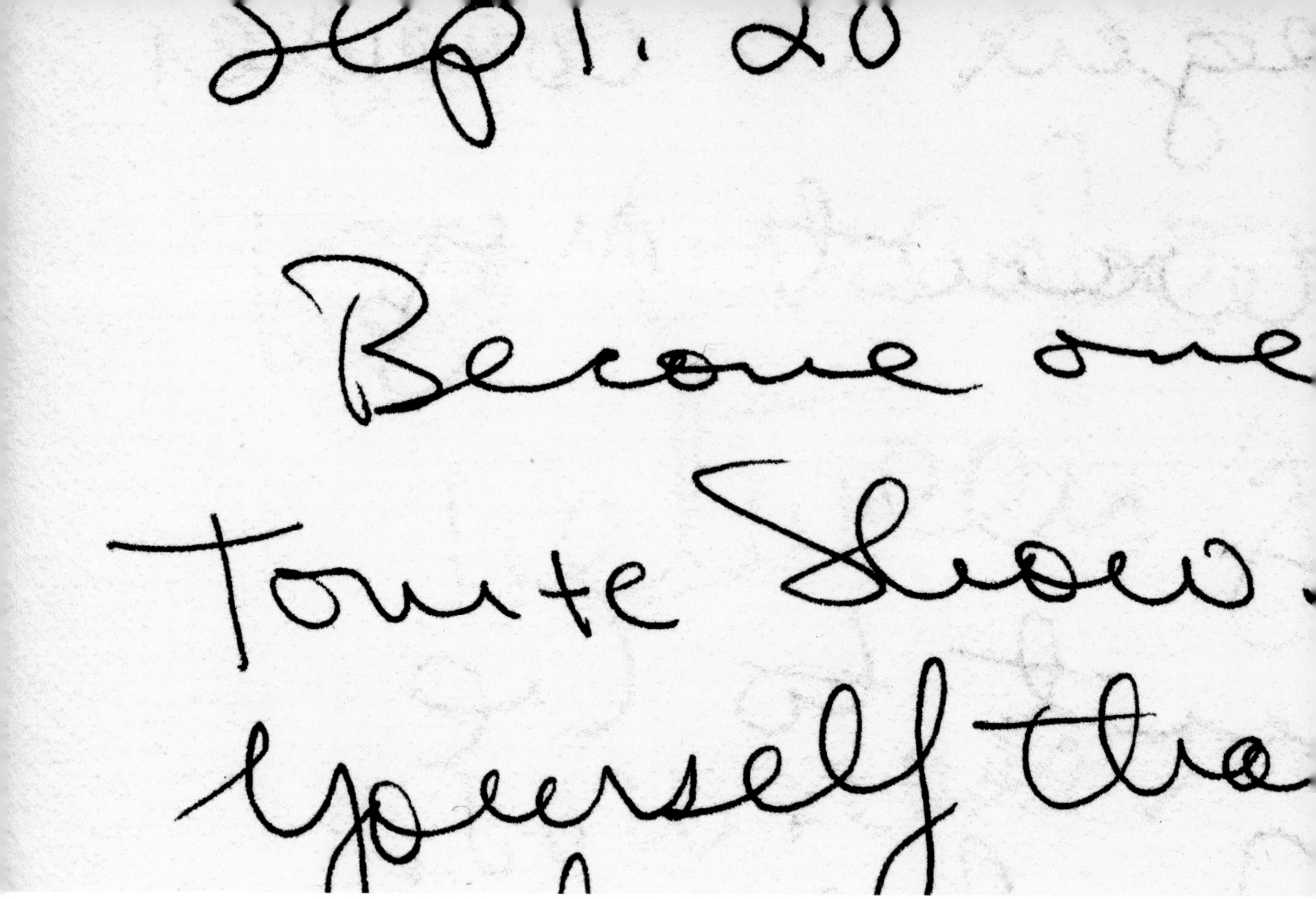

Sept. 20

Become one

Tonite Show.

yourself the

GARRY What I wrote in my journal before hosting *The Tonight Show* the first time is "Just remember to become one with *The Tonight Show*." There was nothing to prove, it was just become one with it and let it happen. That's always been my approach.

6:30

will—die

Be more

lver,

1981

LEWIS SMITH He killed it, and they asked him back. But you would think we would end up with strippers or hookers in some hotel somewhere—it was just him and I alone again at the end of the night. It was just him and I, and he looks at me and he goes, "Yeah, my fucking life is still fucked up. You're still here."

HEEERE'S GARRY!

After years of amateur nights and discotheque venues, Garry's breakthrough set on *The Tonight Show* led to bigger crowds, bigger marquees, and bigger laughs. But even as he started opening for established stars (and becoming one himself through repeat *Carson* appearances) Garry always strived to be more Garry than ever.

In 1983, a teenage Judd Apatow called Garry at his hotel room in Lake Tahoe and interviewed him while he was waiting to perform his next show.

JUDD What would be an example of how a piece of material got thought of, and how it developed?

GARRY Now, I'll tell you an interesting story. I do this joke in my act that I've heard every excuse for a woman not going to bed with me. I think I've heard them all. I remember this one girl actually said to me, "Look, not with this Falkland Islands thing." And I said, "That was over a year ago." And she said, "I still haven't gotten over it yet." And I said, "Well, I can understand that, Mrs. Thatcher." Now, I could tell you about the derivation of so many jokes. Because some of them take literally a year from the time I get an idea to the time I get the line exactly right. And I'll tell you what I'm working on, after this—I'll tell you a real current one. But with the Falkland Islands joke, I got the idea when the Falkland Islands were going on, is it about two years ago now?

JUDD Yeah.

GARRY I actually wrote a joke where I used to come out and I used to say, "Boy, I'm just not meeting any women. I don't know if it's this Falkland Islands thing or what?" And then as time went by I changed it to "I've heard every excuse for a woman not going to bed with me. I remember this one girl said, 'Not with this Falkland Islands thing.'" Which is very hip, and it gets a laugh. And I was telling David Brenner that joke, and David says, "Then you oughta say, 'That was over a year ago,' 'cause that's funnier." "Well, that was over a year ago." And then I said, "She still hasn't gotten over it yet." And then later came the tag of "Well, I can understand that, Mrs. Thatcher." So it just kind of kept going, you know. It just kept going over time, that joke.

Being professional is making a commitment to work — to try your best each time you perform. Being professional is not giving up — quitting or not caring.

And it's not working not committing — remaining unattached — yet working and giving and committed all together into one solid continuing performance and non-performance.

1978

119

Commit to the performance.
Be you. Be funny. Have
energy. Do a great show.
Kill where it's appropriate.
This is not the place to work
on new material.

Commit to this tour. Think
of nothing but killing. Don't
talk to the audience except
when it's necessary. These
people have never heard
your material before.

April 5
The tour has gone great.
More myself than ever.
Continue to focus on doing a
good job on these gigs. Kill when
possible.
Eat well, sleep, no sugar,
exercise and meditate. Less Excedrin.
Don't think about money or
career.
It's Spring!

I turned
thirty and
I'm kind of
depressed
about it,
because it
was three
years ago.

Concerning your act.
less Jewish jokes. More
writing and digging deeper—
more than just jokes.
As for performing—go for it
each time—commit on
the stage—CARE! Not
caring is a cop out, its hiding.
Be a pro. Take the next
step.

1982

OAN
VERS

... perhaps the hottest comedienne in
... returns to Caesars Palace for the
... year.
... sauciest and quickest wits in the
... s considers no topic untouchable
... y above her scathing and hilarious
... he beautiful comedienne spares no
... erself. She's likely to crisscross the
... ng ringsiders about all aspects of
... lives and then throw in her own
... ences for contrast. Her monologues
... ations of marriage and embarrassing
... necologist are audience favorites.
... book, "The Life and Hard Times of
... witz," is currently high on best-
... e book has already inspired a Joan
... ecial for Showtime, which was
... t Caesars Palace March 14-17.

DOC
SEVERINSEN

Though most closely identified with the "Tonight
Show," on which he has been the trumpet-playing
musical director since 1967, Doc Severinsen is also
so outstanding in his instrumental field that he's
been voted Top Brass no fewer than 10 times in
Playboy's prestigious annual music poll.

A much-in-demand nightclub star, he also headlines
several weeks each year in Las Vegas and Atlantic
City, where, besides playing brilliant trumpet, he
delights audiences with his singing and comedic
flair.

Doc's career began in Arlington, Oregon when
his father, a gifted amateur violinist, urged him to
learn violin. Doc insisted that he wanted to play the
trombone, but settled for a trumpet, which was the
only horn in the local music store. Thus began a
career which finds Doc on the Circus Maximus
stage tonight.

GARRY
SHANDLING

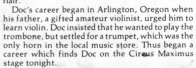

Garry Shandling recently entered comedian
nirvana when he hosted the "Tonight Show." Just
as it was for George Carlin, Bill Cosby, David
Letterman, Joan Rivers and David Brenner, to sit
in Johnny's chair is synonymous with being
recognized as one of the great comedic talents.

Being the guest host on the "Tonight Show" was
an emotional pinnacle for Garry that certainly
justifies his switch away from a lucrative TV
writing career six years ago and even for not
becoming the electrical engineer he started out to
be in college. "My goal is not to do anything that
isn't true to who I am," says Shandling. "What I've
spent years doing is shedding any artificial technique so that the Garry you see on stage is the
same as in the living room. I am not out to become
a show business personality." Garry writes all his
own material, most of which is based on daily
experiences which are then adapted to his style.

DAVE COULIER Suddenly you're getting the premium spots at the
Improv and The Comedy Store and you're a big deal. And you
suddenly get elevated amongst the comedians to this status of "Oh,
that guy's on *The Tonight Show*." I went to his house one night and
Donna Summer was there. I was like, "Oh, you guys are friends too?"
Then he became friends with Doc Severinsen, and suddenly he was
on this career path that was just exploding. And it was really fun to
be his friend too, to see your friend have that kind of success that
he's been dreaming about forever. And he enjoyed the challenge of
coming up with the next set. Of, you know, pushing the material.
Because his goal was to be sitting in Johnny's seat, hosting that show.

Sept. 30
More work lies ahead.
The realization tonight that
one doesn't stop growing. The
mistake I've made in the
past is that I be been trying
to grow towards a goal. There is
no goal. This is it. This is life.
The growing is life.
I followed Richard Pryor
tonight and was intimidated.
Commitment., . Maturity.

Oct 2 or 3
I love my cabin.
Finished a very unusual
week at the comedy store.
Followed Billy Crystal,
Richard Pryor... Robin Williams
went on after me. I was
intimidated. They have a
confidence. Or rather
I was thinking too much.
I felt like an amateur.
It all comes with time. It's
here now! You don't have
to search for confidence — Just
don't think and it's there.

One month after his *Tonight Show* spot, Garry was learning to hold his own, sandwiched between heavyweights like Richard Pryor and Robin Williams.

Heeere's Garry!

I said to my doctor last week, "My penis is burning." He said, "That just means someone's thinking about it."

GARRY It's just odd that sex crosses my mind with my first *Tonight Show* appearance. I think that probably it's a great metaphor for the import that it is, and that's what I always hoped, equally after sex, that a woman would say I could come back another night. Then I became a regular guest, and I'm telling you, I'd be driving around in Los Angeles thinking, *My God, I'm like a guy who's a regular guest on* The Tonight Show. *Look at me!* I couldn't believe it. I'm not kidding, I actually thought, *I'm the comedian who does* The Tonight Show.

More than a full year before he would fill in for Johnny, Garry already had his eye on the prize.

March 24, 1982
Never stop working on your act. Never sit back. Always dig deeper. Focus on your work. Develop material faster. Prepare for guest-hosting. Assemble material quickly, be yourself, be less dirty. Do tonite shows closer together. Always try to be more honest and funnier. <u>Feel</u> where you're at. <u>Be</u> where you're at.
Don't be jealous over other's success.

March 26
<u>I will never be upset over career or money</u>. I am what I am and have what I have. I am not and don't have.

1982

123

BOB SAGET Garry liked to practical-joke me. And I was a vulnerable guy. He had been opening for Donna Summer. He couldn't come to my wedding because he was opening for Crystal Gayle, and understandably. But he had some really good steady gigs where his stand-up got stronger—that's where he became a bona fide 'nother level of comedian. So he had all these new people in his life, and he invited myself and my ex-wife, Sherri, to his house in the Valley, Tarzana. And he said, "It's a costume party, so make sure you're in costume." And we got there and everybody was waiting for us and we were the only people in costume.

Heeere's Garry!

GARRY I don't know where, what year in the '80s, I was opening for Joan Rivers in Vegas or something and I don't know how this happened. We're standing by the side of the stage and I don't know how it came up, but she brought [the car accident] up. She said, "You've never told me about that experience." And I stand there like a fool and I tell her. And I said, "But you know, I don't talk to anybody about it." And she walked out—you've got to give her credit—she walks out onto the stage at Caesars Palace, and this is her opening: "You know, Garry Shandling had a death experience. Let me tell you what happened." And she only goes a little ways and then the joke is over.

1983

Don't get angry at being on the road so much - accept it - it is what is right now. you're doing it. Give yourself credit for what you've accomplished lately:

10th Tonite Show - which they said was the top two or three ever done.
Killed in Las Vegas, Atlantic City and the Universal Amphitheatre in L.A. And in every other city.
Toured this summer with Donna Summer, Joan Rivers and Melissa Manchester.
Pitched a show to Carson Prod.
Have been more yourself on stage than ever. Feel much and more solid - even in front of 10,000 people.

Garry got to know Joan Rivers not only by opening for her but as cohorts and guest hosts on *The Tonight Show*.

Oct. 31 —

Get back into work.
Dig deep. Write and talk
about what you want.
Be funny. Have fun.
Talk about things that go
on in life.
   Write funnier stuff
than ever before. This
is done by writing stuff
that's truer than ever.
   Stop wondering.

1983

I once made love for an hour and five minutes. Well, it was on the day you push the clocks ahead, but I don't think she saw that.

127

QUALITY INN

The most comfortable place...under the Sun.

PLEASE CHECK THE APPROPRIATE BOXES AND GIVE US YOUR FRANK OPINIONS OF OUR SERVICES AND FACILITIES. YOUR COMMENTS WILL BE KEPT CONFIDENTIAL.

1. WAS YOUR RESERVATION HANDLED PROMPTLY AND COURTEOUSLY?
   Yes No Comments *I was told to leave my room one hour after moving in.*
   ( )(X)

2. WAS YOUR RESERVATION ACCURATE AS YOU REQUESTED IT?
   Yes No Comments *I had requested another Hotel.*
   ( )(X)

3. WAS THE SERVICE OF OUR BELLMAN FRIENDLY AND COURTEOUS?
   Yes No Comments *He spit on me and then called me a Jew.*
   ( )(X)

4. WAS THE SERVICE YOU RECEIVED AT THE REGISTRATION DESK PROMPT, FRIENDLY AND COURTEOUS?
   Yes No Comments *I had to wait 3 days at the desk and was told I couldn't go to the bathroom*
   ( )(X)

5. WAS YOUR ROOM CLEAN, PLEASANT, COMFORTABLE?
   Yes No Comments *There was dog shit in my bed.*
   ( )(X)

6. WE WOULD WELCOME ANY COMMENTS YOU HAVE ON OUR RESTAURANT, BAR OR COCKTAIL LOUNGES.
   Comments *Have them taken out.*

7. DID YOU RECEIVE FRIENDLY AND COURTEOUS SERVICE FROM THE

	Yes	No		Yes	No
Bellman	( )	(X)	Valet Service	( )	(X)
Maid	( )	(X)	Room service (phone)	( )	(X)
Telephone operator	( )	(X)	Room service (waiter or waitress	( )	(X)
Cashier	( )	(X)	Laundry Service (phone)	( )	(X)
Credit Office	( )	(X)	Assistant Manager	( )	(X)

8. IF ANY MEMBER OF OUR STAFF PROVIDED OUTSTANDING SERVICE, WE WOULD WELCOME AN OPPORTUNITY TO COMMEND HIM, OR HER, ON YOUR BEHALF.
   Name *I wish.*

9. AS A FINAL THOUGHT, HOW WOULD YOU CHANGE OR IMPROVE SERVICES OR FACILITIES OF THE AIRPORT QUALITY INN TO BETTER SUIT YOUR NEEDS AND DESIRES AS A GUEST? *New Walls. Beds and toilets would be nice.*

Optional Name *Lester Maxwell*
Business Address
or
(over)

BOB SAGET There was a gig once where Garry got paid all in cash. I believe it was a Canadian job, but it was U.S. dollars, and he and his manager had to stuff their pants with it, and there was no TSA. So here they are, scared to death, both of them stuffed with Garry's cash, as they're going through security. And just laughing their asses off at "What are we doing? Are we garment salesmen? We just sold what, contraband?" And all that happened was, Garry did a show.

My friends tell me I have an intimacy problem. But they don't really know me.

Nov. 21

Watched Steve Wright
at comedy store. Funny
guy. Some competitive
feeling swelled up — this is
normal. But in all
honesty, I felt his is
a style I can not only
write, but have,... and
recently performed it as
Eddie Landers. To do
Such hip material (or "Bizarre"
material, you have to lock
yourself into that style
slightly irregular
i.e., a comic, delivery
irregular material — and it
will work.)

1982

Heeere's Garry!

Sometimes I feel alone in what I see and believe I don't want to feel jealousy or envy. I felt some. But I know what I saw — a bright guy able to write funny lines. No insight at this point. No honesty at this point. But Woody was the same.

Paula Poundstone is very, very funny — there's a person there. That's what makes me laugh — the person. Good material makes me say, "That's funny."

Belzer makes me laugh. I think I have a great understanding of styles of comedy and how to write for each.

The difference in his style is that it is him. That's how he is. When you do it, you "assume" that character. There is no choice but be willing to be what you are. You are going, and leave gone, a completely different route. You have to work harder for a longer period of time. Your style is "Garry" — a little more confident host-type, funny in the everyday-way Garry is funny — as "natural" as possible. You've spent years getting rid of contrivances to make it pure. Your path is also a unique one.

More importantly — what does all this matter I'm life — in the universe — striving for your own purity is all that is important — and I think that's what you're doing thru your stand-up. You don't want to know anyone who would like you more or less dependent on how good your career is going or how much material things you've got. You won't be any happier if other comics envy you or praise you. These are outside sources.

To be yourself.

You can die a hot comic — big deal.

A set photo from *Alone in Vegas*.

ALONE IN VEGAS

Alone in Vegas was Garry's very first stand-up special. Made for Showtime in 1984, it was mostly a distillation of Garry's stage comedy at the time, but accompanied by something new: a series of conversational, fourth-wall-breaking vignettes that paved the way for the meta-goofery of *It's Garry Shandling's Show*.

GARRY It was a very broad twenty-five minutes of stand-up. But then, also, the other half was the technique where I talk to the camera and took the audience with me. To me that was the interesting part of starting to explore something deeper about the medium and playing with it a bit. And it ultimately led really to my first series, where I talked to the camera. Which is not unique. Woody Allen did it in his movies, and I was certainly influenced by that. And I was not influenced by George Burns, who was before me, because I was too young to remember his show, but in hindsight, he talked to the camera.

> I'm single. Those of you who know me, I'm very lonely. I belong to a group called "Sex Without Partners."

Above: Garry first performed this joke in 1985 on NBC's *Michael Nesmith in Television Parts*.

I have a new house. I sold my old house for $85,000. My landlord was real upset about it.

Did any guys do this, shoplift salamis when they were kids? You go into a grocery store, you put one in your pants, and you walk out. Because no one's gonna stop you and go, "Excuse me, is that a salami in your pants?" If they do, right, you just go, "Well, thank you very much. I'm pretty proud of it myself."

A friend of mine just got divorced and he had a divorce party. They showed the wedding film in reverse with the couple walking away from each other.

I just broke up with my girlfriend because she moved in with another guy. I said, "That's where I draw the line."

FROM THE COUCH TO THE DESK: GARRY HOSTS *THE TONIGHT SHOW*

Heeere's Garry!

On August 24, 1983, Garry made his second
leap in late night when he was given the
keys to *The Tonight Show* for the very first
time, promoted from guest to guest host.
Over the course of the next half decade,
Garry would take over Johnny's chair on
thirty-nine occasions.

My mother wants me to have kids, just not with other people.

Work harder on material. Give more than 100%, Work to do a Tonite show sooner. Give more than 100%.

Never again think that you have little time left. Never think again of the concept of time. Keep a clear mind for eternity. There is no time. Now is infinity

1983

PETER LASSALLY (executive producer, *The Tonight Show*) It was the only show, really. There weren't eight other late-night hosts. For comics it was their dream, and their career, if they hit it off on the first appearance. And if Johnny would call you over on the couch, you had it made.

JIM McCAWLEY
THURSDAY
APRIL 11, 1985
HOST: JOAN RIVERS

GARRY SHANDLING

WHAT DO YOU DO WITH YOUR TIME OFF?

He went on vacation to Hawaii. Hit on the stewardesses, learned to ski, stayed at a friend's house in Hawaii, has baby jokes.

DO YOU OWN YOUR OWN HOME?

He bought a Porsche instead, it helps with girls. Has girlfriend jokes -- a routine about the stewardess -- oyster jokes, etc.

DO YOU HAVE RULES ABOUT DATING THAT YOU FOLLOW?

Has a couple of them, and will lead himself into a long run of house jokes and realtor jokes.

Joke prompts for an appearance on *The Tonight Show* with Joan Rivers as guest host.

GARRY I remember being upset later, my fifth or sixth time, that Johnny still hadn't asked me over to the desk. By the time he did ask me over to the desk I was within weeks of them saying, "Do you want to guest-host?" Carrie Fisher had preceded me and was talking about her parents, Debbie Reynolds and Eddie Fisher. And I sat down and I said, "Maybe you know my parents, Irv and Muriel Shandling?" And that made him laugh real hard. And I think that's where he decided to give me a shot. Because it was very organic.

Heeere's Garry!

July 11

Tonite show in a couple of days. Just be Garry. Don't let material clog up your head on panel. I'm a club there no pressure because you feel you can handle any situation and will come up with the material when you need it. Also you are willing to risk. There is no reason to sit at panel if you're going to do jokes. It's not you. The reason you're doing this is to be yourself. Just relax and have fun.

1982

LEWIS SMITH Carson had already asked him over to the chair a couple of times to talk, and he'd killed. And he had his jokes with Carson. Because you really couldn't come over and really *talk* to Johnny. Johnny invited you to get a couple of laughs; he didn't invite you over to really talk to you. A lot of comedians would make that mistake, but Garry knew that immediately. Goes, "I gotta have these jokes ready, 'cause I know he expects me to get a laugh." Sure enough, once Garry got the laugh, Johnny would go, "Well thank you, Garry, for coming over." But that's the intelligence of him. He was always pretty situationally aware of what had to be done.

GARRY (to Carrie Fisher) It's hard meeting new women. I'm happy to meet you. Your parents are Eddie Fisher and Debbie Reynolds. Maybe you know my folks: Irv and Muriel Shandling?

JOHNNY CARSON (laughing) Irv and Muriel Shandling?

I have a mirror above my bed and, on it,
it says, "Objects are larger than they appear."

Never compare. Each time you catch yourself comparing on any level - STOP. Each time you compare remember each is perfect in his own way. A real good looking guy was given that as his edge. Everybody has strengths and weaknesses. But there are no weaknesses. Each is perfect.

Comparison is neurotic.

STOP

Aug 16

My real goal in life career-wise is to host the Tonite Show.

1983

I'm not sure "goal" is the right word. Rather, what I'd really like to do if I could do anything is host the Tonite Show.

When I am one with God I am goaless, desireless, calm, happy, content, fulfilled.

I am burned out now, and need to go to the cabin and rest, and meditate. I can't think of any jokes for awhile.

As I continue doing Tonite shows, I must look like more and more as a host - as the host.

In this same way - become more and more like

GARRY I'd done my first *Tonight Show;* it went well, as a guest. So I said to my agent, "Is there any shot that I could guest-host?" And she said, "Get that out of your mind. Just get it out of your mind. That's never going to happen." Because Letterman was the last person, which was probably two or three years prior to that, and they're not going to have any new guest hosts so just don't think about it. It's not in the cards, it's not possible. About two years later the phone rang and they said, "Albert Brooks just canceled. He was supposed to guest-host *The Tonight Show* tomorrow night. And they want you to do it." I can't remember the last time I had a reaction where I froze—I was panicked, my hands were shaking, and I said yes.

Take each thing for what it is.

March 26

When I talk to David Steinberg or Buddy Mora they say I need to create a project or I will reach a dead end.

The question to myself is, "am I being lazy - should I be doing this?"

I think the answer is yes, but you have focused on the Tonite Show - they have called to you about guest hosting, so you rightly so have been working on another set. I think it's time to make another commitment. Do your next Tonite show, Have a strong set, and great panel - feel like a host. Look good - work out - there's nothing less attractive than a fat stomach.

DAVE COULIER He called me up and he said, "Dave, I'm gonna host." And I knew exactly what that meant. And I said, "I'll be right over." And so I drove over to his house. I just said, "Man, this is amazing, it's happening." And that was the only time I saw him really nervous. He was really nervous about that.

Heeeeere's ... Garry Shandling?

Comedian Garry Shandling will replace Johnny Carson as host of the "The Tonight Show" while Carson takes time out because of an eye infection, a spokesman for the late-night talk show said.

"After that, we are going on a day-by-day basis," said Joe Bleeden, publicist for the show. Bleeden said he was not familiar with details of Carson's ailment.

Shandling, who hosted the program in 1983, will appear tonight and possibly tomorrow.

— from staff and news service reports

JUDD What was it about Garry that made you think he could do it?

PETER LASSALLY His energy. The audience loved his monologues. And I wanted to try it. I was very lucky that the show was a big hit always, so anytime there was interference or suggestions from the network, I'd say, "Okay, I'll talk to Johnny about it." And that was the end of it.

How many have seen me before? Applaud. Now how many have never seen me before? Applaud. This is the happier group, it sounds like.

CHUCK SCHUMACHER (Garry's friend) I went with him every time until I moved in '90, and you could see him getting his legs. He was getting so confident and handled the guests really well. I got to see some of the backstage dysfunction which led to *The Larry Sanders Show*.

GARRY I usually carry my notes with me. I always make little notations. And my friends who do imitations of me and make fun of me always say, "This is Garry . . . this is Garry before a show: 'Excuse me, I'm busy.'" And I have these wadded-up notes that I look through because I write constantly.

PETER LASSALLY Five minutes before showtime I'd walk into the dressing room, and [Ed Solomon] and Garry would be sitting on the floor of the dressing room with little scraps of paper, and I'd say, "Jesus, guys, do you have to work till the last minute?" And the answer was yes. But it made me frightened, because it was that way every time.

JUDD What kind of preparation would you do for the show? I mean, you're interviewing people, which is new to you. Plus you have to have a ten-minute monologue okayed. How did you go about preparing all that?

GARRY It was interesting because I hadn't worked in about twelve days—which is a long time for a comic to go without working. Because you don't keep your chops up on the stage otherwise. So I assembled a monologue of material I had done before—there was nothing else to do. And I went out to two clubs that night, tried to figure out what I wanted to do for my monologue. And just tried to get my feet back on the stage, because I hadn't worked in nearly two weeks.

Phone interview between Garry and a teenage Judd in 1983.

"Continue not struggling. One cannot host the Tonite Show struggling each night Become one with it.

1986

GARRY I was sitting behind the desk and then I realized my first guest is Joan Embery from the San Diego Zoo, who brings on an elephant into the middle of the stage. And I'm just holding on to that desk like, you know, I'm at sea and this is my life raft, and at least I've got this that's solid. And I walk over and I realize the elephant was here and Joan Embery from the San Diego Zoo was on the other side of the elephant, and she was making him do tricks.

And I was shouting across the elephant. You can still see it on tape—I shout for about a minute and a half before I realize I'm on the wrong side of the elephant. And I just make some move to get on the other side. I'd written some jokes, and I'm a good ad-libber. I'm good on my feet, so to say. There I was on my feet, and I said, "Well, Joan, what tips do you have for, you know, other elephants that might be watching who want to get into show business?"

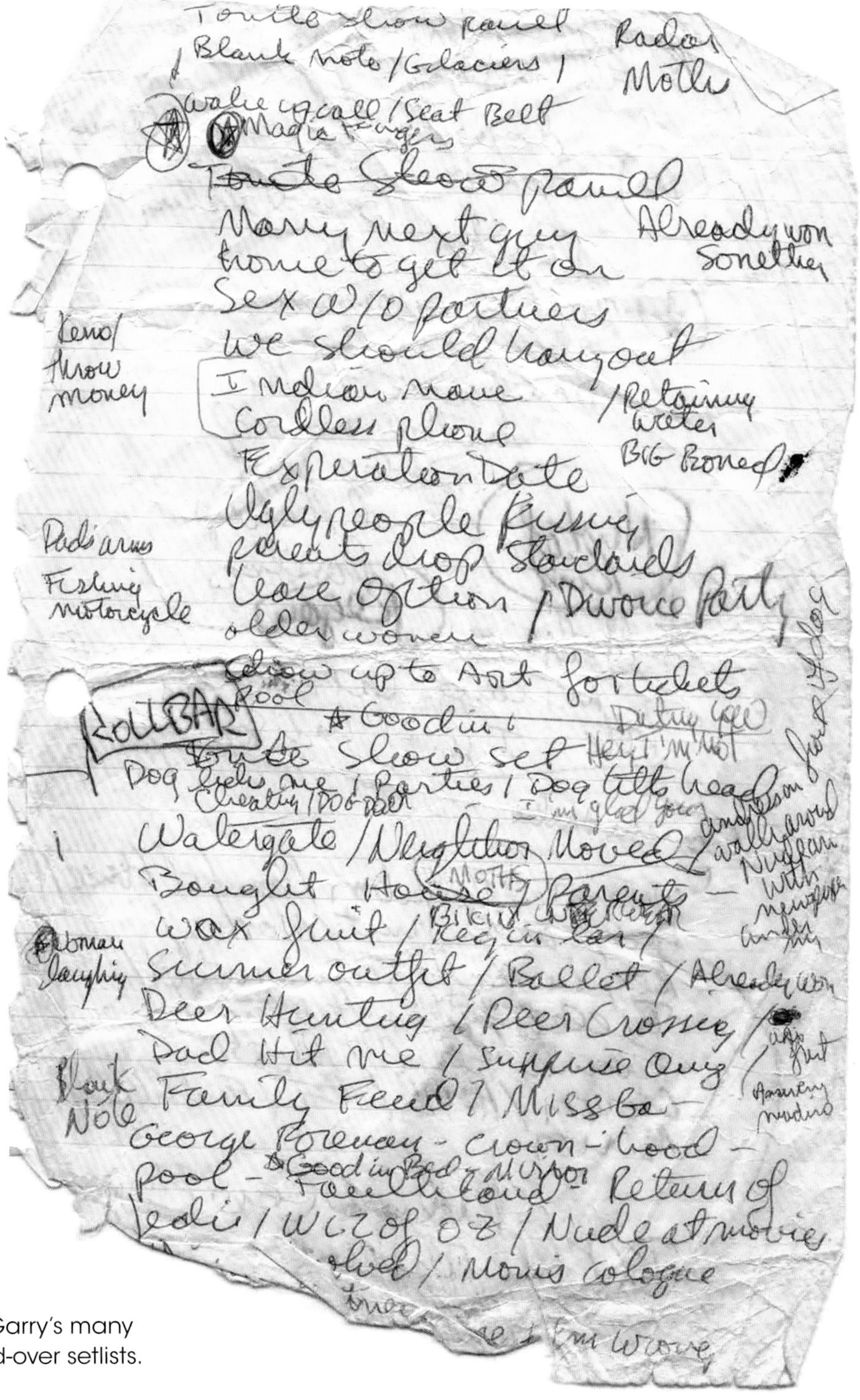

Tonite show panel
Blank note / Glaciers
Wake up call / Seat Belt
Magic Fingers
Radar
Moth
Tonite Show panel
Marry next guy
Already won something
Home to get it on
Sex w/o partners
We should hang out
Indian name
Cordless phone
Retaining water
Big Boned
Experation Date
Ugly people kissing
Parents drop standards
Dad's arms
Fishing
motorcycle
Lease Option / Divorce Party
older women
Reno / throw money
Show up to Art for tickets
Pool
Good in
ROLLBAR
Tonite Show set
Dog licks me / Parties / Dog tilts head
Cheating / Dog
Watergate / Neighbor Moved
Bought House / Parents
MOTHS
Wax fruit / Keg in car
Woman laughing
Summer outfit / Ballet / Already won
Deer Hunting / Deer Crossing
Dad Hit me / Surprise Quiz
Blank Note
Family Feud / Miss Ga
George Foreman - crown - hood -
pool - Good in Bed - Mirror
Faceland - Return of
Jedi / Wiz of Oz / Nude at movie
olive / Mom's cologne

One of Garry's many scribbled-over setlists.

1986

The Garry Shandling Show's
25th Anniversary Special.
2 years longer than
the Tonight Show

THE GARRY SHANDLING SHOW: 25th ANNIVERSARY SPECIAL

After only a handful of *Tonight Show* guest-host spots, Garry was already looking for a way to deconstruct the late-night format. In 1986, he produced this comedy special for Showtime, a deadpan parody twist on anniversary clip shows in which Garry played a longtime host alongside his sidekick, played by Paul Willson. The special was replete with fake reminiscences and flashbacks, including a profane interview with Mr. Ed and guest spots from Donny Osmond, Señor Wences, and the legend himself, Johnny Carson.

Sketch – Casting a new
Mr. Ed. Horse on couch
Guy asking horse what
he's doing later.

GARRY I had done one special for Showtime and they said come in and pitch another one. And I was in the bathroom in the building where Showtime was and I thought, *Well, why not do an artificial twenty-fifth anniversary special?* But it just struck me, and I see in hindsight how these pieces of the puzzle fit together, because here's a guy who's pretending like he's hosted a talk show for twenty-five years. And I thought, *I know I can pull that off and make it look real.* It just happened. I mean, the idea just came up out of the blue. In the bathroom. Where not very many good ideas come up.

You've got to remember that Johnny never did anybody else's anything! So the fact that he said "I'll do something" meant *I like this guy*. It meant he respected the talent. I mean, if I thought about it too much I would— It wouldn't be what I do.

PAUL WILLSON For one thing, he was making fun of twenty-fifth anniversary shows and self-congratulations and that kind of thing. But I think if you look within the individual bits in that show, you see that a lot of it is just not good, or it's strange. It's just "Why am I watching this?" kind of stuff. It just expressed his idea of what those shows add up to, which is really not very much.

I like the bit with the porno cards, that was pretty funny. And with Donny Osmond, that was fun too. But I think the most fun for me was just the back-and-forth between Garry and me. I sort of understood guys like Ed McMahon better, because it's not that you shouldn't top the top dog, the top banana, it's that you can't. You just aren't able to. Because there's a reason they're the top banana. Garry's sense of humor, it was low-key. But it was very powerful and you had to be in the boat with him in order to do it, and he was always at the rudder. It was really sort of amazing to watch.

GARRY I still don't think I'm near my potential.

JUDD You feel you have a ways to go?

GARRY Yeah, I don't think the things I'm doing on the stage now are what I'll be doing five years from now.

JUDD What will you be doing?

GARRY I hope that it'll be even more honest than it is now, more personal. Because it takes time for people to get to know you. I mean, Richard Pryor is the perfect example. If you look at what he was doing ten or fifteen years ago, it's different than what he does now, because we *know* him. He can just get up and start talking about his life—and that's the funniest stuff.

JUDD So you feel if you are more familiar with people and more famous, your comedy will develop also with that.

GARRY I wish that word "famous" didn't have to be used. I think that's a real drawback for comics when they try to be famous or even think about that. Because it has nothing to do with the comedy. But when people get to know you, certainly, it's just like in life, when people know you they're a little more comfortable with you and you can talk about different things.

JUDD What are your long-range goals right now?

GARRY Well, first of all my long-range goal is to be funnier. It really is. And to get better, and to keep digging inside myself. Number two, I guess, is to find the right vehicle, either on television or film, that'll allow me to be funny in the way that I'm funny.

Then, really
develop an idea, a
show that allows
Garry to be garry,
A show where you
talk to people, can be
funny, can be positive,
Can bring positive ideas
and attitudes, have
fun.
  Don't fall into a
routine out of laziness.
    To host the
tonite show, you

The comic

Story of a boy from the midwest (small town) who
comes to Hollywood to become a comic. The pitfalls,
the changes in his life, the changes in himself
as he struggles to make it in a world that is totally
strange to him. The one thaing that drives him
is his love of his work. He dicovers talent isn't
everything, and that agents, producers, writers,
other comics are not how they appear on the surface,
always waiting to steal from the other guy and
from him. He goes through a metamorphisis and slowly
changes to be like them. When he becomes successful
he relaizes he has become everything he once hated.
It xxxrix drives him into a suicidal state for he
can no longer stand himself. Now he wishes he was
back in his small town. Eut it's too late. Now he
is trapped withing himself and the world he has
c reated for himself. Now he must perform -- a
driven man looking for the love he is missing now,
asking every audience to excuse him. Asking himsllf
to excuse him. But it is too late. Too late.

An early TV show idea of Garry's.

4-6-75

3 Fools at
Susie's Birthday Party   6-3-75

THIS IS THE CHAPTER ABOUT GARRY'S SHOW

The book is almost halfway finished—how do you like it so far? In 1986, Garry flipped the idea of a sitcom inside out with his first game-changing TV series, *It's Garry Shandling's Show*, a metafictional multicam that took a smirking sledgehammer to the fourth wall. Airing for four seasons on Showtime, and later in an edited form on Fox, the show continued Garry's tradition of mining laughs from self-awareness, becoming a cult hit in the process and influencing an entire generation of upcoming comedy writers.

I realize that I don't go to the woods or meditate as an escape. I have nothing to escape from. My career is going well. I'm July I will start to tape Garry Shandling's Show on Showtime. I'm off the road until that's completed. It will be hard work, but I believe it can be a funny, unique show. I have been very bored with my stand-up and not pleased with my work. Nevertheless I get more and more job offers. My new house is coming along and is very liveable, and

1986

GARRY NBC was very interested in me doing a sitcom. So I went in to NBC and I said I'd like to do a sitcom where I play a comedian and I have a platonic girlfriend and it's just about my life. And they said, "No one's going to watch that. Do you have to be a comedian?" And I said, "Well, I'm not going to refer to it like in an inside way. It's just that I'll be relating to people and life, and that's what I do for a living. It's not going to be about me consumed with which club I'm working or anything." And they said, "No. Could you be a hardware salesman?" I remember

This Is the Chapter About Garry's Show

this really well. And I said, "I want to talk to the camera." And they said, "No, no, no, no. You can't talk to the camera. Can you talk to a dog?" It brought back all my memories of writing sitcoms, which I'd already done. So I didn't need to write another sitcom. So Showtime said, "We'd give you a series for anything you want." And no one knew what Showtime was. No one knew what cable was. But I heard the phrase "you can do whatever you want" and that's what I jump on. So women should know that if they want to have a relationship with me, that's the key phrase.

May 27

Well, I will be hosting the tonite show starting Monday for one week. Then another week July 14. And my ~~First of all~~ ~~Showtime~~ series will begin to shoot July 28. First of all — my recognition factor will change. Probably go up. This has nothing to do with your work or who you are. You are the same whether you're recognized or not. Do not become what you are on T.V. You are not your job.

Your path is it, To keep the mind pure. To let go. As regards the Tonite Show, The strength comes

ALAN ZWEIBEL (co-creator, *It's Garry Shandling's Show*) Garry and I came up with the idea for *It's Garry Shandling's Show*. I wanted to do a modern-day *Dick Van Dyke Show:* a guy with a wife and two kids who was a comedy writer who spoke to camera. Garry told me about this idea he had where he played himself—a comedian named Garry Shandling—and spoke to camera. So we were on the same wavelength that way. We combined [those ideas] and said, "Okay, fine, let's see what we can do together." It was taking what was the standard form and turning the dial a little bit on it, coming at it from a different angle. Garry, knowing the form of situation comedies given his background of *Welcome Back, Kotter,* had a certain love/hate relationship with what was the norm. We grew up with the norm, but it was time to put it on its ear just a little bit.

ALAN ZWEIBEL When I first met Garry, I'd seen him on some talk shows, and I thought he was funny but I didn't know what to expect. One o'clock in the morning, the phone rang in the hotel room and I picked it up. "Hello?" "Alan, it's Garry." I go, "Hey, man, what's doing?" "Alan, my dog's penis tastes bitter. You think it's his diet or what?" I called my wife. I said, "I think I found a writing partner."

AL JEAN (writer, *It's Garry Shandling's Show*) It was inspired by, to a degree, the old Burns and Allen show. Not to give it enormous credit, the Shandling show, for being completely original. It was about a guy who knows he's doing a television show, so he's like, "Well, this is my best friend, Pete, you were gonna meet his son, Graham, we haven't cast him yet." That was a joke on his show. And he could do anything—he could switch continuity, he had I think a dream hat that he could put on and go into dreams and stuff. All the shows in the '80s were usually the three-camera format, pretty standard. So this was such a breakthrough.

GARRY The writing process on *It's Garry Shandling's Show* started out right. Alan Zweibel and I wrote the pilot in like a week in the Parker Meridien hotel. Just sat there and banged that thing out. And we sent it to Showtime and they were actually blown away by this script.

JOEY CARBONE (composer) They asked me to write the theme song, so I met with Garry and Alan Zweibel. Garry said, "I don't want the typical kind of theme, like *The Mary Tyler Moore Show*, where they talk about the show." He said he wanted it "light on the spice." He came in with the line *"This is the theme to Garry's show. / I don't really want to write it / But his mother knew my mother."* I started thinking about it on the way home and came up with the melody in the car.

ALAN ZWEIBEL We wrote the theme song in an elevator. This is when I knew that we were meant for each other. We were in an office building in L.A. I think it was 9200 Sunset, because that's where Bernie Brillstein and Brad Grey had their offices at the time, and they were on an upper floor. And we get into the elevator, and Garry says, "You know, I'm gonna need a theme song." And I said, "Yeah, what do you think it should be?" He said, "What if we do a theme song about a theme song?" And I go, "Well, what are you saying?" He goes, "Well, *'This is the theme to Garry's show, the theme to Garry's show. Garry called me up and asked if I could write his theme song.'"* And then I said, *"I'm almost halfway finished, how do you like it so far? How do you like the theme to Garry's show?'"* And then he said, *"'This is the theme to Garry's show, the opening theme to Garry's show, this is the music that you hear as you watch the credits.'"* Then I said, *"I'm almost to the part where I start to whistle, and then we'll watch* It's Garry Shandling's Show.*'"* We both started whistling. And then one of us said, *"'This was the theme to Garry Shandling's show.'"* Doors open. We're in the lobby. We looked at each other. We got a theme. "It's been a full day, I'll see you tomorrow." It was magic.

Characters

Garry - an asshole

Platonic Girlfriend - has an asshole

Pete - married to an asshole. Has two
kids, each with an asshole.

Lewis - a reformed rabbi.

Garry's mom - mother of an asshole

From the Television Series "It's Garry Shandling's Show"

IT'S GARRY'S THEME

Lyrics by
GARRY SHANDLING
and ALAN ZWEIBEL

Music by
JOEY CARBONE

1. This is the theme to Gar-ry's show, the theme to Gar-ry's show. Gar-ry called me up and asked if I would write his theme song. I'm al-most half-way fin-ished. How do you like it so far? How do you like the theme to Gar-ry's

neena!

IT'S
GARRY
SHANDLING'S
CAMERA.

Canon

It's Garry Shandling's mom: Muriel is put to work on the set of her son's show.

Garry and
co-creator
Alan Zweibel.

SHOWTIME PRESENTS
IN CONCERT
AT CELEBRITY THEATRE
'IT'S GARRY SHANDLING
LIVE' TOUR
THUR JULY 21,1988 8PM

CONAN O'BRIEN (late-night host) *It's Garry Shandling's Show* came out—it was the perfect time for me, because I had just moved out. Greg Daniels and I were both twenty-two, neither one of us wanted to go out to L.A. alone, we were scared, but we said let's go out together. And so we went out together, and we got a job at *Not Necessarily the News,* and we lived in crappy apartments, and I had a 1977 Isuzu Opel. That I had bought at the airport, that was beat up, for like four hundred dollars. And that was this period of my life where I was just obsessed with "What are the good shows?" There were so few good shows back then. So when that show came out, it was kind of a revelation. Really funny, breaking the fourth wall. I had been kind of a nerdy student of comedy, so I remembered thinking, *This is cool.* I remembered going over to our friend Rob LaZebnik, he's a *Simpsons* writer now, and we would all of us watch *It's Garry Shandling's Show* together. And be delighted that there was something like that. People take it for granted now. Go back. You'll be stunned at how little good comedy there was, and really the kind of comedy that would inspire a twenty-two-year-old comedy writer who was aiming high. And so Garry Shandling was doing the work, in the '80s, that showed everybody, *This is what can exist.* And that was back when it didn't exist anywhere else. And so that was a big deal. Very much up there with SCTV before it— a show that's telling you, *This can exist. This is being made for you.* That's how I thought, that's how it felt to me. Like this is being made for you, and this is proof that this kind of show can exist.

'It's Garry Shandling's Show,' and it's terrific

It's Garry Shandling's Show
Showtime
Tonight, 8:30 EST/PST

TV PREVIEW
BY MONICA COLLINS

A horse is a horse, of course, of course. And when Garry Shandling horses around, he looks like Mr. Ed — buckteeth, shaggy mane and watery brown eyes.

Sometimes, when he laughs at his own jokes, Shandling throws his head back and whinnies. You see all those teeth and you want to stuff a carrot in his mouth to reward him for being so funny.

Shandling's half-hour comedy should air on network TV so more of us could see it. For now, *It's Garry Shandling's Show* is an obscure gem.

To watch it — back on Showtime in a new batch of episodes — is to suspend disbelief.

Garry reminds you every moment that it's only television.

All the sitcom trappings are there — the comfortable living room, the friendly supporting cast, the amusingly bedeviled star. But once you hear the theme jingle — "This is the theme to Garry's show" — you know this is a different breed.

Shandling never breaks the audience connection. When we're presented with the "central conflict" (Garry knows all the TV terms) of this episode — his Guatemalan maid will be deported unless she marries a native — our star turns helplessly to the camera. "I know what you're thinking. You're thinking this is the show where Garry marries the maid so she can stay in the country."

He promises that won't happen. But it does. And his friends applaud his decision: "Compared to the game-show bimbos you usually date, Maria looks like Eleanor Roosevelt."

Garry looks puzzled: "Eleanor Roosevelt? Isn't she on *Card Sharks?*"

It's Garry Shandling's Show is the funniest TV-conscious show on television.

MIKE REISS (writer, *It's Garry Shandling's Show*) The show was so well regarded in its time, and won all the CableACE Awards you could fit in a truck, and then it's almost forgotten. It's almost forgotten, just because he so eclipsed it with *Larry Sanders*. But at the time, anyone would have been happy to just have that first sitcom.

AL JEAN When I met my wife she said she was a fan. I said, "Of *Larry Sanders*? She goes, "No, the first show." I go, "The first show!" It was like, *Oh my God, I love you.*

GARRY That show was just balls-out funny. I don't think we ever tried to make any deep meaningful life point. The theme itself was the structure of the show, which was breaking the conventions. I mean, there was some clever stuff. We let the audience vote on what I should do in the story. I think it changed things because it was like bringing it all out, all the conventions out, and saying, "Here's how it works. Usually by this point you marry the housekeeper so she can stay in the country. Do you guys think I should do it? Because I'm not so quick to get married." And they would vote.

Aug 11

Become one with
my show. No seperation
Expect no results. Expect
nothing back. To do
just to do is the highest
spiritual path.
         Never attach importance
to results — only the doing.
Remain nothing during
the doing.

1987

PLAYBOY Your show's main set is a replica of your house in Los Angeles. When you made that decision and then realized it would be seen by millions of people, did you have any second thoughts about your interior decoration?

GARRY No, I was just pleased that you couldn't see the street address from the inside of the set. I thought it might become confusing, two lives that meshed in an abstract sort of way between reality and the show. But I've never lost track of who I am. I've never caught myself talking to the cookie jar instead of the camera or making love to a woman and suddenly looking up for the red light, thinking, *Are we on?*

		12:30 P.M.					
11 G.I. Joe				**18** Dennis the Menace		drama. (90 mins.)	Bridge t
40 Inspector Gadget		**4** Chance of a Lifetime		**40** Centurions		**40** Kojak	Conclusio

'Wall' breaching leaves some viewe

By Guy MacMillin
Newspaper Enterprise Association

On a recent episode of Showtime's "It's Garry Shandling's Show," Garry's maid, Maria, told him that he was going to be deported to Guatemala.

Then several friends, who'd apparently been watching the show at home, stopped by Garry's house to offer advice. Somebody suggested that Garry marry Maria so that she could stay in the country.

Garry wasn't sure what to do, so he took a microphone and walked out of his sitcom house, right past the cameras, to ask people in the studio audience.

Their opinion was divided. One woman said she didn't care whether he got married because her family didn't get Showtime.

Shandling's odd little sitcom deliberately blurs the line between show business and reality. It's sort of an extreme extension of "Moonlighting," where the actors often remind us that they're making a TV show. In one Christmas episode of that program, even the dead crooks came back to life to join the cast and staff in singing carols.

Garry Shandling

This isn't new. In the '40s and '50s, Jack Benny had a weekly radio show about a guy putting on a radio show. George Burns took the practice to TV, stepping out on the porch to talk to viewers. Woody Allen has done it in the movies. Audience participation in the theater dates back to Shakespeare.

More recently, advertisers started using the trick. Remember Lloyd

Nolan and those dreadful Supe Poli-Grip commercials? He'd tell what great stuff it was, then he'd sa "I don't need this script," and he give us what was supposedly the rea scoop on denture stickum. All th while, the director would yell, "O clusive seal, Lloyd!" and "Cut! Cut!

Reality caught up with Nolan, wh died, but last year the ads we back, word for word, featuri Claude Akins.

The technique has a name. Sho time calls it "breaking the four wall." That's the imaginary wall b tween the performer and th viewer.

Of course, the supposed asides the audience are all part of th script. The wall can't really be br ken unless somebody actually go berserk on TV someday and do jump out of a sitcom at us. Un then, Shandling has to be considere the master of the art.

The Tucson comedian opens eac show, which airs 9:30 p.m. Friday with a monologue in his living roo or kitchen, talking to "you at home He announces his theme song — hilarious little tune.

A few weeks ago, when his neig

RADIO

unsteady

ors came over and were about to iscuss a marital problem, Garry's 'iend Nance said, "Let's give them ome privacy." "Yeah," Garry said, we'll watch on the monitor." And ey did, walking right past the edge f the kitchen to find it.

There's something refreshing bout a TV show that you don't have o pretend is real. Sometimes you an feel pretty silly pretending to onder whether "Stingray" will get way from the bad guys every eek.

But I hope other TV producers on't rush headlong through the ourth wall after Shandling. After ll, researchers say that people who atch a lot of TV already have a ough time telling fact from fiction.

It's known, for example, that eavy viewers tend to overestimate ne amount of violent crime in so- iety, and they underestimate the ercentage of women who hold pay- ng jobs.

If we get too many programs like nandling's — with nobody quite re what's real and what's not — ome poor folks out in television nd might get so confused that ey'll go right over the edge.

REVISED
8/4/86

SCENE ONE

FADE IN:

INT. GARRY'S LIVING ROOM - DAY

(GARRY ENTERS THROUGH
FRENCH DOORS)

APPLAUSE

                    GARRY

(HE UNPACKS A COUPLE OF
THINGS)

Hi, welcome to the show. I'm really gald you're here, because I think of you as more than a viewer; I think of you as a friend and I'm happy you tuned in, because now I have my own show, and I just broke up with my girlfriend. My friends always say "there are plenty of fish in the sea." What does that mean? What do fish say when they break up? "Don't worry about it, there's plenty of chicks on the beach?" So, I'm moving in here. I just sold my old place for $85,000.00. My landlord was real upset about that. He said "You were renting" and I said "Okay, I'll give you some of the money."

                    (more)

JUDD How good a comedy writer was Garry?

AL JEAN Oh, I think he was one of the funniest guys that ever lived. I mean, I've been around a lot of really funny guys. Garry was right at the top of the list.

THE SHAND-LINE

OFFICIAL NEWSLETTER OF THE GARRY SHANDLING CABLE TELEVISION PROGRAM

SECOND SEASON OFF TO GOOD START
—GREY OPTIMISTIC—

This week, an exclusive chat with Executive Producer Brad Grey, from his car phone.

SHANDLINE: Are you excited by the 54 show pick-up?
GREY: Wait a sec -- I just want to get in the left lane.
SHANDLINE: Are there any guest stars lined up yet for this season?
GREY: Let me just get around this idiot in the Mercedes. I think he's drunk.
SHANDLINE: Thank you for speaking with us.

ELVIS' GHOST WATCHES OVER CONSTRUCTION

The Shand-line has learned Elvis Presley's ghost is walking the grounds of Sunset Gower Studios, supervising building improvements. Production staffers Terri Bahr and Jerilyn Ryan saw the spirit early this morning barking orders at workmen on the scaffolding.

"He was so close," says Terri, "I wanted to reach out and run my fingers through his hair."

The ghost hopes to renovate the studio to resemble Graceland, his home in Tennessee.

"He's the King," says newlywed Jeri, "whether on stage or mixing cement." Watch out, Bruce Ryan! Sounds like Jeri is "all shook up!"

A MESSAGE FROM SANDY WERNICKE

I'm sorry I haven't had a chance to come by yet, but I hear everything's going well. Keep up the good work.

Sandy Wernicke

Sandy Wernicke
Executive Consultant

ALAN ZWEIBEL Gilda Radner's last TV appearance was on *It's Garry Shandling's Show*, and at the time they believed she was in remission. And she had such a good time doing the show and she was feeling sort of strong. There were meetings that Garry, Gilda, and I had with Michael Fuchs, who was then running HBO. And Garry was going to create a show for HBO for Gilda in which Gilda played the star of a variety show, à la Carol Burnett or anybody who's the star of their own variety show. And we would show her at home, and show the offices. Now, I'm not saying that this was the genesis of *The Larry Sanders Show*, but when that show didn't happen because Gilda passed away, it made perfect sense that Garry did *Larry Sanders*.

GARRY When that door opened and it was Gilda Radner, you could feel the energy. And it was really moving. She was sick during the taping. Alan was very close to her, and I think it was difficult for him. You'd taken a really truly emotional moment like that, of a woman with that kind of heart, being on the precipice of dying, and going on a show and saying, "Garry, I have cancer. What's your excuse?" On camera. That's what you want to—God love her—explore. That's what you want to explore. *Let's do a show about this.* You know, hard to go back to the other stuff. And she had a blast. So for her that show functioned great because she just wanted to have a blast and be back on TV. And she did.

LIVE FROM NEW YORK . . .

On May 16, 1987, Garry vaulted over another comedy milestone, hosting *Saturday Night Live*, with a monologue full of classic stand-up and a self-referential first sketch in the style of *It's Garry Shandling's Show*.

Stay in the moment,
each moment. Commit to
Characters.
    play 105%
Satisy yourself.
Entertain the audience.

MAR. 7
    on May 16 you will
be hosting Sat Night.
The thing to be is myself.
Be funny and work to write
some material that's special.
To do my best work. ∞

Sketch —
 Talk to camera - Lorne
Michael stops you.
 Weird
 Japanese
 Cool asshole
 Sexist
 Paranoid about Aids &
  disease
 Japanese Comic - repeats monolo
 Singles Bar Language Album
 Doctor who thinks Blushing is
  a disease. Bypass
 Talk show host

May 8
 Sat Nite Live
is next week. Remain
Loose. Have fun. Be funny.
Have fun. Commit to
working. Have fun.
Concentrate and write
during the week. Work
extra hard. Sacrifice.
Then you have 2 or 3
weeks off.
 Remain yourself.
Have fun. Rehearse and
work hard as though
it was your show.
By Sunday you'll be done.

1987

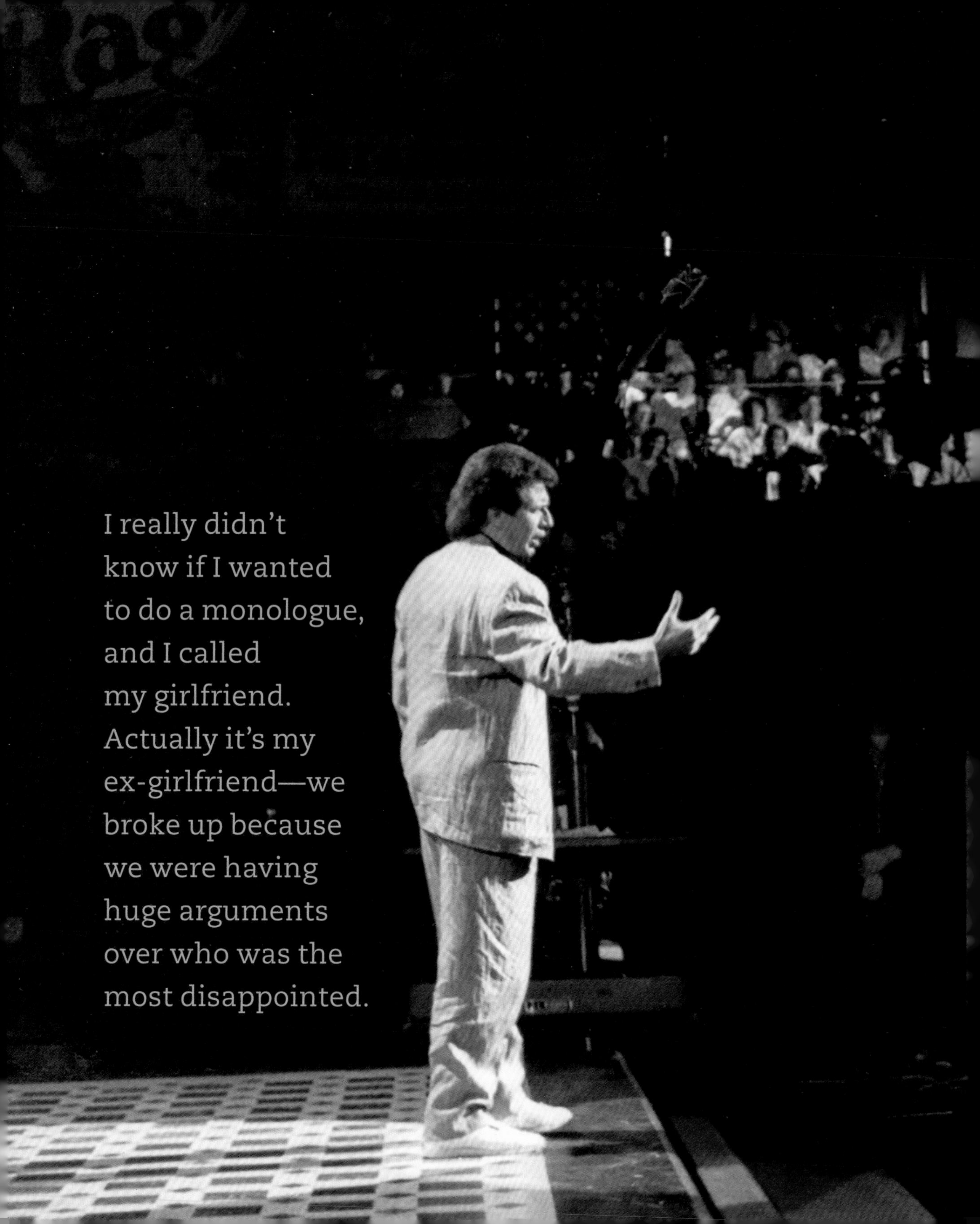

I really didn't
know if I wanted
to do a monologue,
and I called
my girlfriend.
Actually it's my
ex-girlfriend—we
broke up because
we were having
huge arguments
over who was the
most disappointed.

NBC TELEVISION STUDIOS
RADIO CITY • RCA BUILDING • NEW YORK

SAT.
16
MAY
1987

WELCOME TO
SATURDAY NIGHT LIVE
WITH
GARRY SHANDLING
MUSICAL GUEST
LOS LOBOS

DOORS

CLOSE

10:40 PM

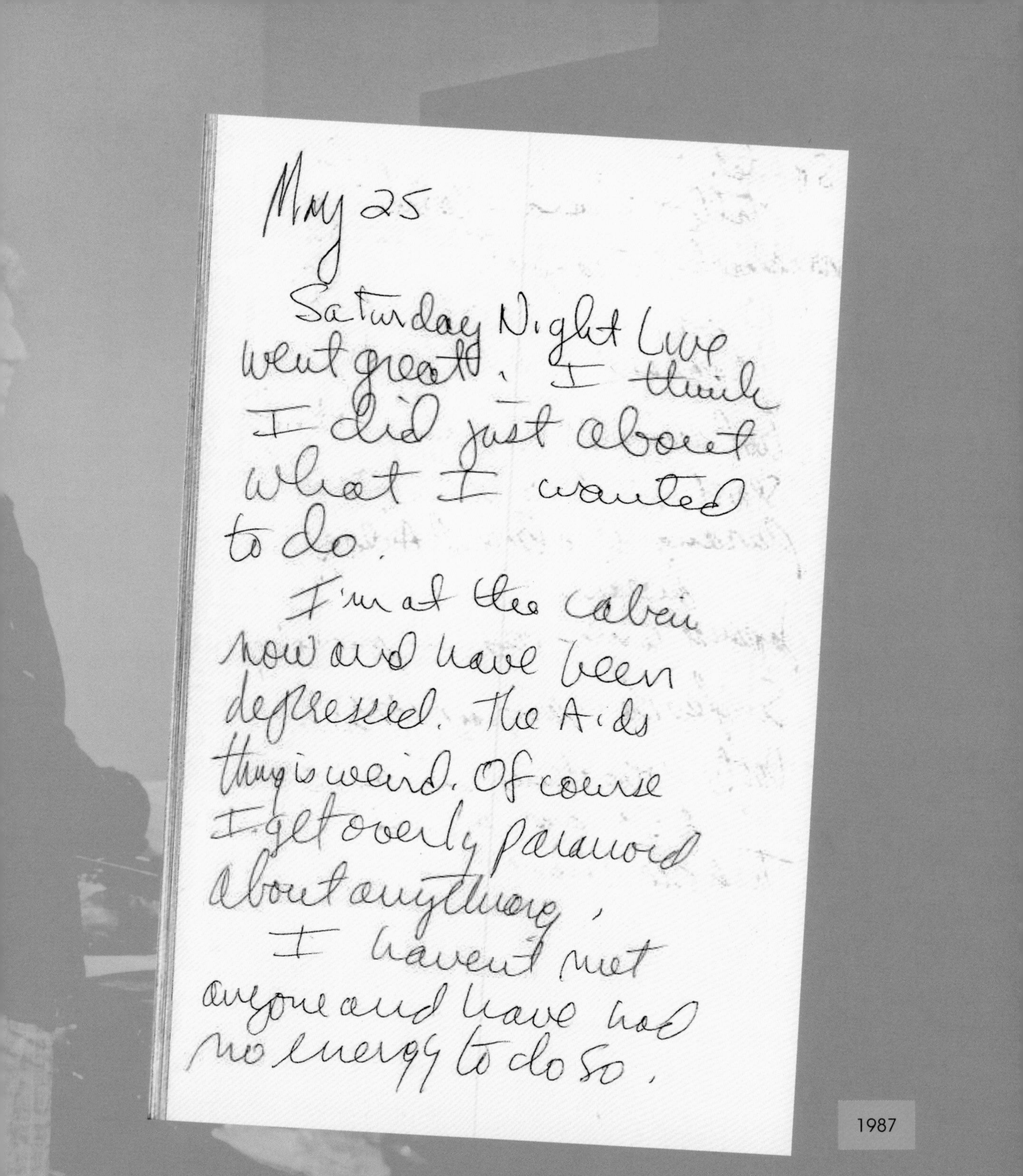

May 25

Saturday Night Live
went great. I think
I did just about
what I wanted
to do.

I'm at the cabin
now and have been
depressed. The Aids
thing is weird. Of course
I get overly paranoid
about anything.

I haven't met
anyone and have had
no energy to do so.

1987

181

ALAN ZWEIBEL There were times we would take a hiatus because Garry was going to guest-host *The Tonight Show*. And I would go with him to the offices over there and I would help with the monologue, and it was grueling for Garry. Because anything that Garry did, it was more than 100 percent. He threw himself into it. So if he was going to guest-host *The Tonight Show* for a week, we would shut down *It's Garry Shandling's Show* for three weeks. It was everything to him. It was all about the work. It was all about the investment of all of his time, all of his energy, of coming off good, and not dropping the ball in any way.

Garry Shandling Monolog -- 8/8/88

The Writers' Strike has ended and these guys are wasting no time.
One writer just sold his picket sign as a movie of the week.

Sports Illustrated has announced it is coming out with a new
magazine for children. Roman Polanski has already put in an order
for the swimsuit issue.

The first cover will be "Babies In Sports", featuring John
McEnroe.

There's been no relief for the drought-stricken farmers in the
Midwest. A N.J. storm blew in, but it was from New York, and it's
been raining syringes for three weeks.

The terrorist group Islamic Jihad has announced it is disbanding.
Some members plan to pursue solo careers while others are going
on tour to recreate their greatest hits.

It's rumored that George Bush is considering Clint Eastwood
as his running mate. After "Every Which Way But Loose", Clint
must figure "I worked with a chimp, I can work with a wimp."

Come to think of it, that's the same thing Reagan said.

I'm going to let go
of my career. let go
of the pressure of my
t.v. show, I'm pitched
up for 3 years, there's
no pressure. Stop doing
this to yourself. Only
you can do it.

May 5
    Why do I feel
so shitty? Is that
old burning neurotic
loneliness. Like I have
no life and reason to
live. My head is tight
and I feel like crying.

GARRY I had hosted *Tonight Show* maybe fifteen times or something, probably. But a week at a time. And I was exhausted after every one of those weeks. Then, like the engineering class, like the *Sanford and Son* scripts, I went, *Do I want to do this the rest of my life?* I was asked to alternate with Jay Leno to be the guest host on Monday nights, or whatever it was. But I had already started *It's Garry Shandling's Show*. I ran the show. So I couldn't run the show, write the scripts, rehearse, and then on Monday night go in. I'm not that guy who could then go in and give 100 percent on *The Tonight Show*. Let alone if I was going to do it every Monday night, or every other Monday night. And I had to call Johnny on the phone and said, "I can't do it." And he'd just gone through the Joan Rivers thing where she didn't call him to say, "I'm leaving to do my own show." So when I called Johnny I said, "It's Garry Shandling, Johnny. I can't host the show." And he said, "Here we go again." And he was totally joking.

This Is the Chapter About Garry's Show

This Is the Chapter About Garry's Show

ED SOLOMON The relationships on *It's Garry Shandling's Show* were super shallow. When you came up with an idea that was from the physics first, the show was too thin, it always failed. But when you came up with a show that was honest and truthful and about something that we as writers, but specifically Garry, could relate to, those shows really held together, and then the physics of the show came later, and that stuff was always really fun. When I was starting out and I was writing TV, people always said, "Try never to get on a show with people who don't have families." Because you become their family. And then you're there till 4:00 A.M. every day. And we were there till 4:00 A.M. every day. Writing, rewriting, rehashing, we were making it up as we went along.

MIKE REISS It was just a long haul. I used to say, "It's fun eighty hours a week." And it was fun, everybody was funny there and he was funny, but oh, the hours were so long. And we used to think, *Oh, it's Alan and Garry, they can't decide anything, it's a hard job.* And then, for three weeks, Garry left the show to do the Grammys, and he just made token appearances, and suddenly we were getting out at seven at night instead of two in the morning, and that's when we realized, *Oh, it's all him.*

This Is the Chapter About Garry's Show

MERRILL MARKOE I wrote an episode of *It's Garry Shandling's Show* too. I wrote a draft of this thing, and then everybody said they really liked it and they gave me compliments, and then they started rewriting it right to the second they were standing on the stage. I remember saying to somebody, I think maybe Mr. Zweibel, "I have a really great idea, why don't you just give the first drafts to the homeless, and then they can get health insurance? And then you guys can rewrite it."

BRUCE GRAYSON (Garry's friend/ makeup artist) I came in the second-to-the-last season, or even the last season. He just felt the show wasn't evolving, and he would talk about it openly. That it was all one sketch tied to another and that there was nothing going forward.

ALAN ZWEIBEL He would wear dark glasses indoors and it was no eye contact, and you couldn't read his face. And so I remember that a lot of energy went into me trying to figure out where I stood with this guy.

GARRY It was very hard to come up with stories about the human condition when we had so many constructs, and there's another word that that show had—"gimmicks." Alan and I always agreed that the show became gimmick-oriented because when we couldn't come up with a story we could rely on being funny. We started to rely on those elements, and we had writers who were hilariously funny with that kind of stuff. And so we started to rely upon that more than the story itself. So after [episode] 65 I was sitting in the editing room one day watching one and I thought, *This has gone past its peak.*

1990

Jan. 3

It's important to ~~remember~~ when looking back on your show to remember the frustration of having to write, act and run the show. The frustration of never having scripts ready. The frustration of not having the energy to commit to acting. The knots in the stomach from not having scripts ready. the monotony of playing the same guy year after year, ~~Day~~ Week after week. the complications of playing yourself.

The bad, sketchy writing.
It is time to move
on. Scary, yes. But the
next growth is as an actor.
To be a great actor, I will
have to get out of my
head and feel. Take
Rorp class. Grow and
mature emotionally.
Get ready by using the
show to grow.
Don't ~~be~~ identify
yourself with your
career. You are you.
You are not your job.
Also, this summer,
work on your stand-up.

"IT'S GARRY SHANDLING'S SHOW."

1. { Leaves + wind
      papers

MAD   2. rehearse w. Newhart TV?

3. shots of audience leaving
       redo end.
       end on nancy w: Gra—

༄༄༄༄༄༄༄༄༄༄༄༄༄༄༄

The last show

༄༄༄༄༄༄༄༄༄༄༄༄༄༄༄

Kim - Death gas
     play out to 2

Birds
⌒ = No gesture
    (keep steve moonlay)

Jessica -
    slow down

Pete - Match

Wednesday
111 Thursday

Final draft
April 6, 1990

ALAN ZWEIBEL Garry was so complex and he was so defensive. He did have a way of getting inside of your head. Lots of times on a show, the show takes on the personality of the star, and Garry was even more so because the energy of the show, the focus of the show, was not only on him, but if you looked elsewhere, you did get the feeling—and I believe that it's true because too many other people vouch for it—that Garry got jealous or angry that you weren't thinking about him or the show. I don't remember him sleeping. His work was his life. And I felt that, as close as we became, to a great extent I was auditioning still. Auditioning as a person.

JUDD To not hurt him.

ALAN To not hurt him. I think there was a mutual discontent of what we were doing together at this particular point. It had run its course. And I knew that Garry resented it. I knew that Garry resented me. And I also thought that what I represented at that time was asking him to be something that he wasn't. I was asking him to be more of me. I wanted him to be something that I can relate to so I can write to it. If his gripe was that Alan's losing focus, that's legitimate.

JUDD Just in terms of having other projects going on simultaneously?

ALAN Also, "I can't edit with you on Sunday, we're taking the kids to Disneyland." What I don't understand, but I believe is the case . . . he also interpreted that personally as betrayal.

195

ore. Goee
nyone
one of
uiet
e the

e is a book
t stages of
ically
more for
lly to
n than
to be

ginal
do not

Compare yourself, your
career, your philosophy
your angeling. Just be.
    <u>Be</u> in your material.
    I notice that this
journal (this specific book)
begins 4 years ago before my
show started. The entry
is April 30, 1986. April 17,
1990 I will tape the last
show. My God, life is
fascinating — it's a flash.
It makes me smile. Time
moves so quickly.
    Stay positive — it's a
switch you can throw.

1991

and want it.

~~It is~~ time to move on.

I would be depressed if I knew now I had to do the show next season.

April 1

Should I buy a house in Hawaii? Try renting a house?

You have very slightly slipped in a couple of areas. First, you have worried a little lately that you don't socialize much – especially other comedians, artists etc... e.g. Rob Reiner and so on. You have also wondered if this means something, like "am I less talented?" can you see how neurotic this is? You used to write the same

FINDING LARRY

It's Garry Shandling's Show may
have revolutionized comedy
by turning the house lights on
its own artifice, but after four
seasons, Garry was left searching
for a new project with fewer
ironic quotation marks. In high
demand as a host and comedian,
he once again set his sights on
conquering a new mountaintop:
acting. At a time when people
were offering him big money to
be himself, Garry wanted nothing
more than to learn how to play
someone else.

Acting is as challenging as stand-up. More so, because it requires you to take an even deeper look at yourself. There will be setbacks, but learn the lessons. 1) Never make the audition bigger than the event in the script. 2) If you have to stray from the script to give it life, choose life. 3) The doing - the emotional subtext - is _flowing_ like music. Lines aren't just delivered. Don't always think, "If this doesn't work out, fine." Don't be afraid ~~to~~ be honest enough to go _directly_ for what you want, without defenses.

3) The words are a vehicle to allow the actor to show emotional life.

4) Do it for yourself, _not_ for the director or the actors. Do what you feel.

As for acting: It is more important to show what you are feeling than being liked.

GARRY (to David Letterman, on finishing _It's Garry Shandling's Show_) We're all done. We did seventy-two episodes, and now I'm trying to decide what I want to do next. But it really left me time to do other things. I'm writing a book—it's called _More Satanic Verses_.

GARRY I auditioned for _City Slickers_. The first read with Bruno Kirby and Billy Crystal went extremely well. I went back a couple days later and had a bad second session. I was really disappointed. I wanted to work with those guys.

DAVID DUCHOVNY (actor) I think he was hurt, in a way, by acting. I think he wanted to be a great actor at some point. At least when I met him, he was interested in doing work that wasn't generated by him necessarily as a comic persona. And I think he thought of that as somehow better. Or more artistic. He valued it in a way that was greater than what his natural gift was for, as an actor and as a comedian.

GARRY The deficiencies I have in my acting are deficiencies I have in my own personal makeup, and I'd like to conquer those. Maybe I should just start studying with Tony Robbins. That's what it sounds like—I really just need some big self-help course.

SPECIAL THANKS TO ROY LONDON

In the '80s, Garry took a class under the tutelage of acting teacher Roy London, and their relationship quickly became one of the most significant in Garry's life. London mentored the likes of Sharon Stone, Patrick Swayze, and Jeff Goldblum, but he fostered a particularly strong connection with Garry, giving him frequent advice on projects and even directing episodes of *It's Garry Shandling's Show* and *Larry Sanders*.

Garry working with London on the set of *Larry Sanders*.

SCRIPT ANALYSIS'

Notes on script analysis based on Roy London's teachings.

EVERY GREAT ROLE IS THE ROLE WHERE YOU ASK YOURSELF, "HOW DO I DO THIS?"

EMPTY OUT FIRST.

START BY LISTING THE FAULTS.

STUDY THE FACTS OF THE SCENE.

BREAKDOWN THE SCRIPT TO GIVE YOURSELF A THROUGH LINE...A MISSION.

BREAK IT DOWN AS HOMEWORK.

BREAK IT DOWN TO BEATS. GO AFTER SPECIFIC ACTIONS.

MAKE SPECIFIC CHOICES BEAT TO BEAT TO MAKE YOURSELF MORE ALIVE.

EVERY CHOICE SHOULD HAVE A BUILT IN OBSTACLE.

FIND CHOICES THAT ARE TERRIFYING AND EXHILERATING, STRONG AND RISKY.

DO THE SCRIPT BREAKDOWN SO THAT THE SCENE HAS THE DYNAMICS OF AN ARC.

AT A DIFFICULT JUNCTURE ASK YOURSELF, "WHAT WOULD I DO IN THIS SITUATION?"

WHEN YOU'RE IN TROUBLE, YOU'D BETTER ANALYZE THE SCRIPT.

BUILD IN THINGS INTO THE SCENE WHICH FEED THAT WHICH YOU HAVE DONE FOR THE FIRST MOMENT THROUGH YOUR PREPARATION.

STUDY A LINE AND FIND OUT WHY THAT PERSON IS NOT **REALLY** SAYING THAT.

SAY, "WHAT IS THE NATURE OF LOVE TO THESE PEOPLE?"

ASK WHY A CHARACTER WOULD SAY ANY SPECIAL LINE.

STUDY THE CHARACTER'S INTENTIONS AND THEORIZE THE OPPOSITE INTENTIONS.

PONDER, WHY DOES THE CHARACTER WAIT SO LONG?

WE MUST LOOK AT THE CHARACTER'S PREVIOUS LIFE WITH CLARITY TO SEE THE PAIN THEY ARE IN.

IF YOU CAN FIND THE WAY YOUR CHARACTER HIDES THE WAY HE REALLY FEELS, YOU CAN BUILD A CHARACTER ON THAT.

WHEN YOU LOOK AT A SCRIPT AND DON'T KNOW WHAT TO DO, THROW THE SCRIPT ASIDE AND ASK YOURSELF, "WHAT DO I NEED TO DO?"

#2) Continue to grow + risk. The next area of growth for you as a person and a performer is as an actor. Work on your acting the way you've worked on your standing, talk-show, sit-com, meditation. I need to allow the ~~power~~ masculine side of me out more. Trust it. Be myself and more trusting, AND COMMITT TO BEING A BETTER ACTOR. COMMITT TO GROWING IN MY CAREER. It is not enough to say it and think it, you must do it. DO.

Yes, there will be steps

1990

GARRY Roy London used to say, "Do you have the courage to discover something new about yourself while the camera's rolling?" And I applaud myself when I do, and beat myself up when I don't.

JEFF GOLDBLUM (actor) Garry and I had found our way to Roy London separately, but I think we are parallel souls in some ways, so it's not surprising that we found our way to him. I met him through Zane Lasky, and he was just starting to help people and coach. I asked him to help me on a few movies, and he coached me. And then I know Garry was a devotee and a student and collaborator. Roy came out of the tributaries of the Group Theatre, and the modern Method acting. Like Stella Adler, you try to render it in the most personal but interesting way. Make choices that were unexpected and interesting.

BOB DUBAC (actor/comedian) In the beginning there was Sanford Meisner, Stella Adler, and Lee Strasberg. They learned their technique from Stanislavski. Those were the three, the beginning of the American theater, teachings and coaches. And then Meisner developed this technique of being authentic and in the moment under these imaginary circumstances. And I think London studied with him in New York, and then when he came out to L.A. found this way to attract and teach certain actors. He had a roster of really famous people that he studied with, saying, "Your own authentic power is good enough. You don't have to act like somebody else." And the true people who had that power—the Brandos, the Clifts, Steve McQueen, these kind of people—they had that energy and that essence within them so much: Don't try to make something fake 'cause it'll never come off as being authentic.

Aug 11? ✰

Roy said the
block — the resestance —
is okay. To Accept
it. It is watching
someone fight
thru that ⊗ block
that is interesting.

The block is fear—
fear of being vulnerable,
fear of looking
silly. sometimes
✰

7 30'92

Now -
I've been working on my acting with Roy, and it will take real discipline to accomplish what I want as an actor and person. I must be willing to feel strongly about what I want and to be willing to discover it. To stay in on a scene. In life, to know what I want and trust it. Don't look for outside approval.

On stage as comedian you made the ~~transition~~ transition from worrying about how the audience was receiving you to taking them where you want. Do the same now

with acting. Be courageous and disciplined. Work harder - be prepared 110%, you learned already there are no shortcuts. Don't get lazy. Don't be less hungry. Love the process.

Don't stop your feelings. Don't control your feelings.

In acting - you're doing and action to get what you want. Then

LEWIS SMITH He coached George Carlin. George, at that level, didn't take the class, really. He took privates. Roy would coach him on his scripts and his scenes. Roy would have people like me come in and read with Michelle Pfeiffer or Geena Davis. And Garry was around for a lot of that.

GARRY He worked every script of *It's Garry Shandling's Show*. He'd have this talk with me every week and he would deconstruct what's happening there and how that applies to your personal life and what are you bringing personally when you're saying that line.

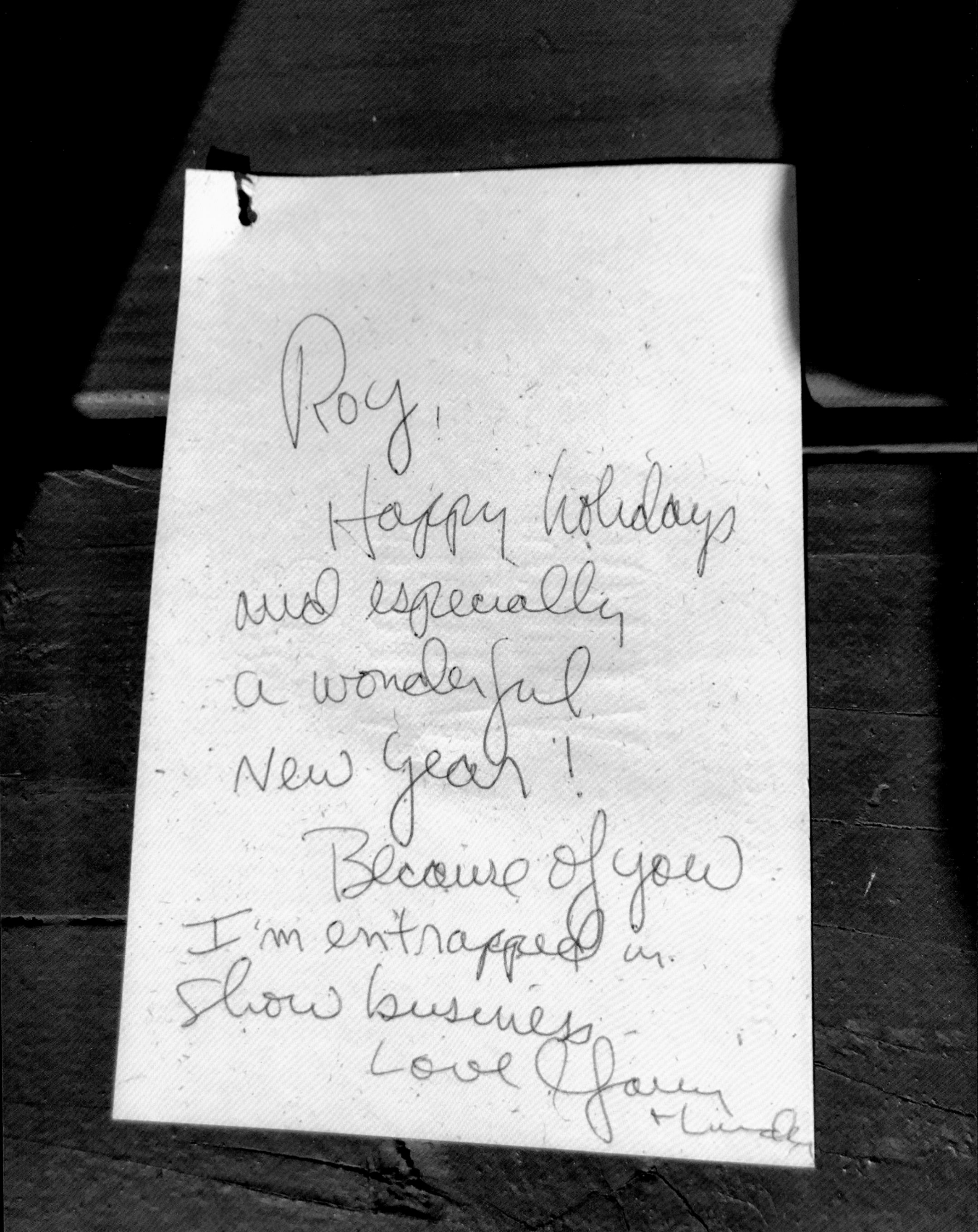

Roy,
Happy holidays
and especially
a wonderful
New Year!
Because of you
I'm entrapped in
show business.
Love Jamie
+ Lindy

You can't do both.

July 17 (?)

Roy London is dying. Who would have thought? How unpredictable is life? This is a disaster. The man I learned the most from—

I love this man and I can't imagine continuing to act without them. I can't imagine continuing a career of any kind in show business without him. I can imagine continuing to live without him. He has been part of me and my life for 13 years. How is this possible?!

GARRY (from the documentary *Special Thanks to Roy London*)

The last thing Roy said to me about acting was "I'm telling you, it's all about love." And when he said it, he was really connected to what love is. It wasn't like . . . just saying it. "And every acting choice," he said, "should come from a place of love." And you could feel how honest that was, and how connected it was.

Finding Larry

JEFFREY TAMBOR (actor, *The Larry Sanders Show*) I know that he loved Roy. And I know I was probably vetted with Roy as well. I think we all were.

GARRY I was a late bloomer. I was confused until I was twenty-seven and started to get into that Roy London mentality. That's when I realized I wanted to take the path of self-discovery, where I could continue to explore this human condition thing we always talk about—because the human condition is hilariously awful.

Aug. 8

Roy died today.

I went to see him at 12:30 this afternoon. He was in an unconscious state, but I spoke to him. I told him that I had come to say good-bye and that it was time for him to go. I told him to let go and stay in the moment — that's all there is. Stay in the moment. Let go. Everyone has a time — this is his. I told him that I loved him and that he would live on in the people he loved and touched and influenced. I told him that I would never leave him. He died ten minutes after I left.

There was the most beautiful sunset tonight — maybe it was Roy.

1993

213

THE HOST WITH THE MOST

After years of keeping Johnny's seat warm on *The Tonight Show,* Garry secured his first major hosting gig in 1990: the 32nd Annual Grammy Awards. It only helped to cement Garry's reputation as one of Hollywood's most coveted masters of ceremony. Multiple lucrative offers for late-night time slots were hitting his desk, and he was faced with a question: Was he a talk show host or an actor? And was there somehow a way to be both at once?

Garry hosted the Grammy Awards for the first time in 1990. He would go on to host them three more times over the next four years.

Finding Larry

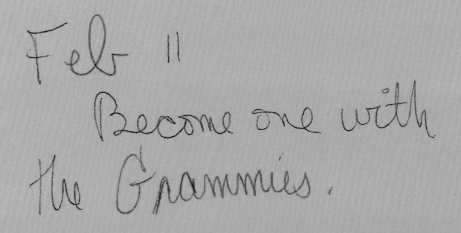

Feb 11
Become one with
the Grammies.

There are advantages to being older. People look at Keith Richards now and go, "He looks good."

I did just hear that Ivana Trump wants one of Donald's big construction projects. So he said, "Great. You can keep your face."

Garry's stage presence was such a hot commodity that even
President George H. W. Bush brought him up for an
impromptu exchange at the 1989 White House
Correspondents' Dinner.

C'mon Garry — Lighten up. Your voice
makes me fade out & focus" Just kidding —
sort of!
Gy Bush

GARRY (from the 1991 HBO comedy special *Garry Shandling: Stand-Up*) A little over a year ago, I'm sitting at my little cable show, which won an ACE Award. I was all excited about that, and then the Weather Channel won one, which put it all in perspective. You know how hard we work to write our scripts? These guys look out the window. "It's, uh, cloudy. Where's my award? Can I have the award?"

So I get a call from this guy at *The Washington Post*. And he says, "Garry, we'd like to invite you to come and sit with us at the Correspondents' Dinner. Every year they have this big banquet in Washington. All the journalists come, and the president comes and does ten minutes of jokes." So I figured, *Okay, I'd like to see that.*

So we get tours of the museums and the White House. You can stand there and look into the Oval Office, which, by the way, is not perfectly round. It's more like an egg shape. When you're there you can see. So as we're looking into the Oval Office, the Secret Service guy who's standing there says, "I just got word: The president is on his way down. If you folks want to stand against the wall there, maybe you'll get a glimpse of him as he walks by." So I'm figuring, *God, that'd be cool, right?*

We stand against the wall. Sure enough, the president walks in with Mrs. Bush. And this is the weirdest moment: As they're walking by, he turns to me and goes, "Garry?" I'm thinking, *Oh, boy, who'd I vote for? Who'd I vote for?* He says, "What are you doing in town?" I said, "Well, actually, sir, I'm going to the Correspondents' Dinner tonight." He says, "I'm going to that! You should come onstage with me. We'll do something together." "Say what, Mr. President?" I actually said "Mr. President." I'd never said "Mister" followed by another nonspecific term in my life. I'm lucky I didn't lose it altogether and call him Mr. Belvedere at that point. 'Cause you're talking to the president of the United States!

He says, "Where are you staying?" I said, "Well, I'm at the Park Hyatt hotel, sir." He says, "I'll give you a call later." (*Laughing*) *Oh, sure you will! I'll be holding my breath, sir.* So I turn and pick my girlfriend up off the ground. She'd been passed out since he said "Garry."

We go back to the hotel, right? We have lunch. Now we're sitting there having lunch in the coffee shop, my girlfriend and I, having this conversation: She's going, "The president's going to call you." I go, "He's not going to call." She goes, "I bet he calls you." "I'll bet he doesn't call me." And you could tell the other people sitting around were going, "Look at these two morons thinking the president's going to call him."

So we finish lunch. I check my messages. Sure enough, there's a message: "Call the White House." With a phone number, which I'm sure is hooked to some answering machine: "Hi, this is the White House, we can't come to the phone right now. We'll call you as soon as this Middle East thing blows over. Bye now." So I dial the number and a man answers. One of the president's aides. I go, "Hi, it's Garry Shandling." He goes, "The president's all excited about this thing." I go, "No, Garry.

Garry Shandling." I figured maybe he thought I'd said, "Dick. Dick Cheney." So he says, "No, Garry, the president's all excited about this." I go, "Are you spiking the president's punch or what?" He says, "No, sir, I'm not." So this guy's a riot, right?

He says, "You know, a couple weeks ago, the president was walking through the tour line and he picked out a couple tourists from New Hampshire, introduced them to the puppies, and it made front-page news. So what the president would like to do is not tell anyone you're there, but he'll say that he was walking through the tour line and he picked out an everyday, average American, just to see what they had to say about the presidency." I said, "This is how he found Dan Quayle, isn't it?" And there's just silence on the phone.

So he says, "Can you come back to the White House?" I said, "Sure, I'll be right there." So now I hang up. We drive back to the White House. Now, this aide meets us in front of the White House, takes us up to the private quarters to the First Family's house. The third floor there, where no one gets to go. Takes us down a long hallway to a den where the president is sitting in short sleeves, by himself, behind a desk, going, "Come on in. Come on in." He's like the warmest, sweetest guy in the world, I swear. If you had an Uncle Bush, this is what he'd be like. I thought he was going to give me a

To Garry Shandling — "Get back in line! Now that you've wowed 'em in D.C." Sincerely, Geo Bush

nickel at one point. He starts showing me around. Shows me the Gettysburg Address signed by Lincoln, and as he's pointing to it, he turns to me and goes, "You know, there's lots of stuff like this around here." *I'll bet there is, Mr. President! It's the White House, sir.*

We talk about jokes, I do the little show, I do five minutes of material. It goes great. I go back to my hotel. I can't fall asleep until like four in the morning, because this whole thing happened in nine hours. What started out as a tour of the White House turned into a *Twilight Zone* episode in my life. So I call the operator in the hotel to put a "Do not disturb" on my phone. At six-thirty in the morning, the phone rings. I'm ready to ream out the operator. I grab the phone. Before I can say anything, she says, "It's the president of the United States calling." I go, "Oh, all right." And he goes, "Garry, I just called to say thanks for doing the show and it was really fun. I'm off to New York now to do some damn thing. . . ." He literally said "damn thing." I went, "Mr. President!" And he says, "Hope to see you again sometime." I said, "Hope to see you again sometime, sir. Why don't you call Gorbachev? Wake him up now, sir!"

A photo that captures the
essence of four late-night
icons: Letterman's guffaw,
Leno's smirk, Carson's grace,
and Garry, looking right at
the camera.

Finding Larry

GARRY I had to make a simultaneous decision. At the point I was offered *Sanders,* I was offered the show after *Letterman.* Letterman had already moved to CBS. So I was offered that spot. And prior to that I was offered the original Conan O'Brien spot. So I had to make a decision, literally, whether to host a talk show on CBS or do a show about a guy who hosts a talk show.

Jan. 4
So I've been
offered a talk show.
It's my decision.
A show could be fun like
the Tonite Show but
with my bend. Stretches
Freeway reports.
Tips on sleeping
Nighttime
Forget about work
what tomorrow
Leave show on while
you sleep.
Guests do stretches.

Jan. 6
I passed on that
talk show!
Oh brother, I
pray I did the
right thing and
that it wasn't
destructive. 2.5 million
a year and complete
freedom. But 5 days
a week - one hour a
day for 3 years and
doing the same thing
I had basically done.
This would have been

a real change in my life. Maybe what I needed. Maybe that commitment to a job and a life.

I got such a knot in my stomach and felt like this was something I should do more than I wanted to do. I didn't want to do it just for the money. I can't picture myself doing it.

When I was getting ready to host the Tonite show, I knew to grow that I needed to be myself on the show — to become one with it, to have fun, to be professional. On my show I worked on my acting.

I didn't know what to work on in this show. To what. Learn to ~~make~~ run the show better. To make it consistent. To be pure.

May 25

One of the things that fragments me, that definately upsets me is that Johnny Carson announced his last show will be the end of may 1992 - one year from now. It's very difficult accepting the fact that I took myself out of the running to be the new host. And that Johnny won't be around anymore! That from now

I can't imagine, so I can't answer. It used to be a goal. I had that weird feeling I could be the guy. I worked so hard at being a host. It's just weird. But goals change. Life is unpredictable.

The choices I've made are me, instead of questioning choice, commit to who you are.

1991

Finding Larry

JAY LENO All comedians have some injustice, either real or perceived. Me, I was—still am—dyslexic. A little. Terrible student. I'm a huge believer in low self-esteem. The only people with high self-esteem are actors and criminals. And if you think you're not the smartest person in the room, then maybe you'll shut up and listen and pay attention. I was always in awe of Robin [Williams] and Garry and Letterman, and my mother always said to me, "You're gonna have to work twice as hard as the other guys to get the same thing." So that worked for me.

One part of it for Garry was that he really thought that he couldn't do a talk show all year, year after year. That he didn't think that he could get up every day and have enough energy. I was always good at simple, repetitive tasks. Every day it was the same—that's pretty easy for me. I like having that. I liked a show every day versus a weekly show because it was literally, you'd write until four-thirty, pencils down, *OKAY, that's it. I gotta go with what I got now. I've given everything I can.* If it was once a week, I would torture myself staying up twenty-four hours a day trying to come up with stuff. But writing, doing it every single day, *Okay, I gotta go over there and do the show, I can't do anything else.* So I actually liked that. I liked the pressure. That was a great thing about *The Tonight Show. The Tonight Show* was like raising laboratory mice. You get a bad batch, there'll be more tomorrow, don't worry about it. Fred de Cordova used to say that the show is never as good or as bad as you think. If you had a terrible show on Monday, by the end of the week you've had four more shows since then. Nobody even remembers.

Aug. 1

A track runner said that they concentrate on their own pace—NOT THAT OF THE OTHER RUNNERS!

Let suppose your past decisions have been right. Bailing out of Tonite show; too much to do at the time. Stopping your show. or clean house— including some actors and all writers, but still

stuck playing Gary Shandling. Turning down a talk show: 42 weeks every night, a lot of jokes.

Just fucking move—on. Don't analyze the past!! Stay clear. Focus on your pace. Grow. Blinders. Blinders.

Garry's indecision over eschewing late night remained even after he had made his decision, but it never settled into regret.

GARRY The reason every episode and the ending credits has "Special Thanks to Roy London" is because when I had to choose between doing *The Larry Sanders Show* or a real talk show, which is an irony, and it came down to that, I was offered a spot at that time after *Letterman* on CBS, which I think Tom Snyder ultimately took at that time. But I was offered that spot, and I

show. The talk
show offer was
a career move and
money. You
began questioning
what your career
was. Instead,
the work is not
yet completed: this
playing of a character
can get better and
deeper - like a play.
Learn again.
Don't compare.

The reason you
turned down the
talk show is: how
could you do
any of the things
you wanted - how
could you continue
to learn. I think
you've got it now.
I really do.

1991

waited to the last second to make up my mind because I admired *Letterman* and I thought that was a good spot to be in and it wasn't too high-pressure to handle. It was a big financial offer. I called Roy London, and I said, "I've got to make this decision, Roy. Am I going to grow more doing this series about a talk show host or grow more doing a talk show?" And I think the decision was made based on I knew that I would struggle and grow more as a writer and as an actor and as a person working on *The Larry Sanders Show*. I knew the philosophy of the creative process in which people were allowed to make mistakes and to play real moments and to risk, and that takes courage. The courage that I needed to find.

A friend of mine said, "You should get married, Garry, you'll get a lot of new comedy material out of it." That's a huge risk. What if I don't?

I'm very loyal in a relationship. Any relationship. Even when I go out with my mom, I don't look at other moms and go, "Ooh, ooh, I wonder what her macaroni and cheese tastes like."

Jokes from 1991 HBO special,
Garry Shandling: Stand-Up

JUDD Years ago, I bought Garry's house. And you should never buy your friend's house, because it gets weird. I almost got killed by Garry. Garry took the *It's Garry Shandling's Show* layout from his real house, so when I bought the house, it was like living on the set of *It's Garry Shandling's Show*. It was in Sherman Oaks, and what happened is there were two chimneys and the home inspector said, "Take this chimney down, but that chimney in the bedroom is fine." Two weeks after I buy it—I'm painting the house so I haven't moved in yet—the Northridge earthquake hits. The chimney they said was safe goes through the roof of the bedroom where I would have been, had I decided not to paint. So, Garry almost killed me.

"EVERYBODY HAS A CURTAIN": *THE LARRY SANDERS SHOW*

On August 15, 1992, the very first episode of *The Larry Sanders Show* aired on HBO. A workplace sitcom, a behind-the-curtain farce, an amorality play, and a Hollywood self-satire keener than a paper cut, the show was an immediate critical success and would cement itself as one of the all-time greats. Garry was able to have his cake and subvert it too, hosting his own late-night show while simultaneously vivisecting it with hilariously brutal precision. Hey now!

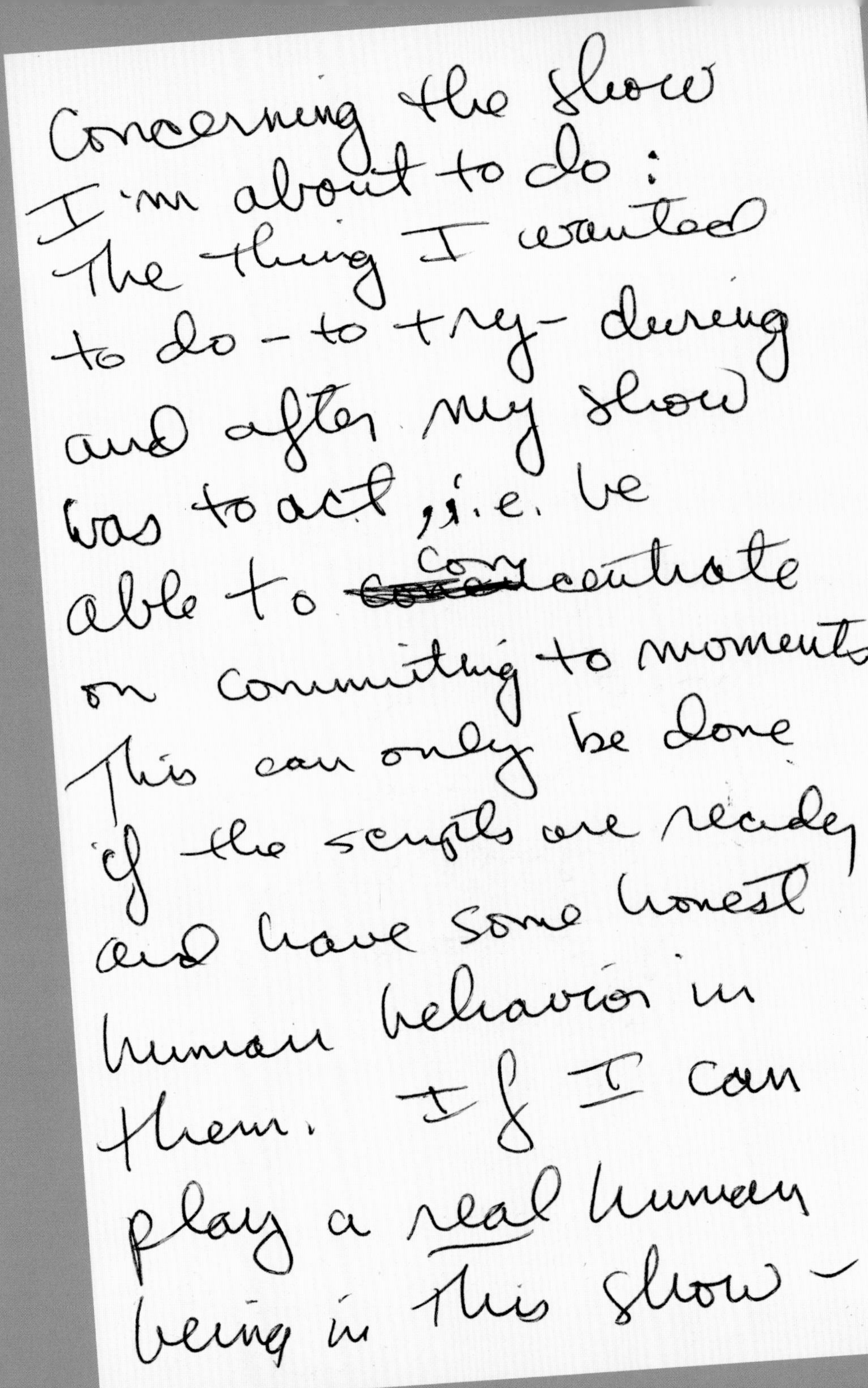

Concerning the show
I'm about to do:
The thing I wanted
to do - to try- during
and after my show
was to act, i.e. be
able to ~~concentrate~~ concentrate
on committing to moments.
This can only be done
if the scripts are ready
and have some honest
human behavior in
them. If I can
play a real human
being in This show ~

GARRY It's about excess. And I would have told you this at the beginning of *The Larry Sanders Show*. It's that I knew that labels put on success were being examined on *The Larry Sanders Show*. Is it successful to be on TV every day? Is it successful to be famous? Is it successful to have a paycheck and in fact what's missing is love and heart, and people are really searching for that?

...not some caricature of Gary — but rather a person who is not "Gary" and who feels what humans feel rather than just go for laughs — that is; create a real character — then I will be successful to myself. This is what I wanted to try, and if it ⊗ can't be in a movie right now, why not do it here? This is

1992

239

Character - that is the next step — it will surprise Everyone — that is the direction of this show.

1992

GARRY There was an episode we did on *It's Garry Shandling's Show* where Garry goes on a morning talk show. And I thought, *Man, there's a story about the people who host this show that I know.* And I always had that in the back: *There's another show here about the person who hosts the show.*

And at that juncture I was offered two other late-night hosting jobs. Because Let-terman had already gone. So those spots at different times came open. The CBS one was interesting to me because I respected Letterman. I had to really consider if I wanted to do a talk show. Again, I had the opportunity. That was a big decision because the CBS offer was an actually big financial offer. And my girlfriend at the time said, "Take the money. Take the

the motivation —
the _real_ motivation —
the creative motivation.
It has nothing to do
with career success,
Cable or network, TV
or movies, talk show
or series, this is
what you wanted
to try. You may
not feel motivated
to write, because
you _never_ wanted
to write again after

your show. Remember,
you were looking for
a movie part that
was already there,
that you could
step into? Remember?
So why should you
be surprised that you
don't feel intense
motivation to invent
another series with
writers, art director,
~~etc~~ etc... You
didn't want to do
all that. Concentrate
on creating a full

1992

money. Take the money. Take the money. . . . Take the money."

I called Roy London up and I said, "Roy, I have to make a decision here. Is there a way that I can learn about myself and the world and people and what this is all really about and get down into that shit and the essence of people's lives and how they cover it . . . on a talk show? Or can I do it on a show about a guy who hosts a talk show?" And then we started to talk about the guy who hosted the talk show and realized that it isn't about a guy who hosts a talk show. It's the ability to have that world within which you could tell the story of human beings.

And so it was never about a guy who hosts a talk show. That show really became a lab for a study of human behavior.

LINDA DOUCETT ("Darlene") The name came about because when Garry finished *It's Garry Shandling's Show* he didn't want to work for a couple of years because he didn't know what he wanted to do. He was turning down hosting, taking over talk shows, like *Letterman*. And he was substituting for Carson and Leno, was stepping in. So he finally found a premise that would inspire him to go back to work, and that was making fun of being a talk show host. I said, "It would be really funny if you could become famous with two people. And you would be Garry Shandling, and then if you name it something that sounds like *Garry . . .*" And he goes, "Yes, Larry Sanders." And so that name stuck. It never changed. And a couple of years later—I think we were in New York City, I think he was hosting the Grammys at Radio City Music Hall— somebody yelled out a cab, "Larry, how's it going?" So we started laughing. It just seemed so incredibly cosmic.

BOB SAGET *Larry Sanders* was full retribution, karmically, for not hosting *The Tonight Show*. Getting to say, "Well, this is what it would have been like had I hosted *The Tonight Show*, it would have been this much of a nightmare. I would have had the sidekick that was this guy who couldn't have been played any better than Hank."

"Everybody Has a Curtain": *The Larry Sanders Show*

JUDD I was a big Jeffrey Tambor fan. I know this sounds funny . . . for some reason, the first time I ever saw you, I thought, *That is the greatest actor. He is the funniest, most interesting actor.* From . . . *And Justice for All,* and then *Hill Street Blues,* where you played the judge. So when Garry said, "Oh, Jeffrey Tambor came in," I was like, "Are you serious? He's my favorite of all time!"

JEFFREY TAMBOR Well, I didn't know that. But, yeah, you really pushed me.

JUDD I think you had it almost instantly, though. I mean, Garry might ask people for weeks, but I could tell, the first time he showed it to me, that he knew it happened. It happened.

JEFFREY We had one of the more remarkable auditions. Garry and I read. And it was that scene, the "Hey now" scene, and Garry was to leave, and for some reason, I picked up the entire couch to block his way. And I remember him . . . You know that look he would do? He looked at Francine, and I went, "I think I just bagged the role."

JUDD But you had Hank the second you started the first audition. That's the funny thing about the audition, is you're completely doing Hank. Like, it's not like it evolved. It was completely there.

JEFFREY My audition is no different than my performance. Which was weeks later. (*Laughs*) You're supposed to get better. It was exactly the same.

"Everybody Has a Curtain": *The Larry Sanders Show*

Beverly sc. 8 chg 2 501

PENNY JOHNSON ("Beverly") First
of all, I wasn't going to audition for it,
because it had been a week of testing for
four other pilots, and I didn't get them. And it was a Thursday
night, my agents called and said, "There's one more show. They'd
like you to meet this guy, his name is Garry Shandling." And I
didn't know who Garry Shandling was. And my husband heard
it, and he says, "Oh my gosh, that guy is really funny. I've seen
him on HBO." And I said, "I don't want to put myself through
that." So my husband asked me, "Please say yes." So I did. And I
went and I met Garry and I met his entourage, and I remember
I saw Jeffrey Tambor in the waiting room. I saw these other girls
who didn't look like me. So I didn't know what to expect. And I
went in and Garry was sitting on a couch, and I was about to
start my audition, and the phone kept ringing. And then it kept
ringing. And I just looked at him and I said, "Are you gonna
answer that?" He said, "No, you can." And I said, "Well, thank
you."

GARRY She didn't skip a beat and she picked up the phone and she said, "Larry Sanders's office," and she took the person's name down and she said something to me like "It was so-and-so" and went back into the scene. And I intuitively loved her. She walked out of the room. The door closed. And I looked to the casting director and said, "Just hire her. Just hire her." And I turned around and said, "Now." She's the most lovely woman there can be. At first blush she might not seem like the edgy comic type that would be adept at improvising, and yet it turned out that she was and always knew her character.

5c.15

SARAH SILVERMAN ("Wendy") He started
coming to see me do stand-up and it was probably like '97 or so. And he said, "I want to do this
on the show where you're a stand-up but you write for the show."
And he had hired my roommate Mary Lynn [Rajskub], who played
Marylou on the show, and he made us roommates. He always
wanted everything to be real.

GARRY I was torn between [Rip] Torn and another wonderful
actor named John Glover. I'd met with Rip and his agent and it
was very awkward. Rip was pleasant but not evocative, and I really
didn't know what to say. Nothing was accomplished and we continued to look for Artie. Then I asked Rip for another meeting.

He came in and I said, "I know that it's inappropriate for me to ask you to read a script, and your agent said you wouldn't read for me. But it would help me get a sense of whether this will work or not." He said, "Well, then, I really don't want to read." I said, "I respect that; let's just forget it." At which point he said, "Oh, to hell with it. Give me the script." He proceeded to blow me away—and nothing short of that. No one saw it except me. My next concern was whether a movie actor would feel comfortable working at a television pace—I thought he'd never done a series. I asked, and he said he had done *Rawhide*. I hired him. Months later, out of the blue, he came up to me and whispered, "You know, I did only two episodes of *Rawhide*." Which explains why he's the perfect Artie—that's Artie's sense of humor.

JUDD I had an interesting relationship with Rip, because I think just the fact that I was there for so long, he liked me. I didn't bother him too much. I loved to chat and hear his old stories. I was a good listener, and I was always proud of the fact that when I asked him to sign my script at the end of the last episode he just wrote, "Judd, you're a good soldier." And I thought, *That's probably the best compliment he could give me.*

GARRY They asked if it could all be on video because it would be less complicated, less expensive. It was very clear to me that the cinematic sense of backstage needed to be filmed and would delineate the two realities, one of which is the outward-looking, somewhat artificial talk show world versus real people backstage. I've said before that the curtain was a metaphor for how we want to be perceived by the public, and then how we really are.

GARRY *Larry Sanders* was about people who love each other but show business gets in the way.

This show is more creatively ambitious than most

other shows. We use both film and videotape. Sometimes there are 6 cameras going at once. We have extraordinary experienced actors who demand material that is honest and

and about characters. We shoot 35 pages in two days and often have to write the script that week. As we all know sitcoms are intensely difficult work — No one would argue the hours. It's a miracle there are any good ones

JUDD It does feel like it was the metaphor for everything Garry was struggling with. His ego and vanity and narcissism and psyche took everything that he didn't want to be in himself and put it in this character. And then mocked it and said, *Isn't this a terrible way to live?*

PETER TOLAN (writer, *The Larry Sanders Show*) Well that's true. I mean, when I think about him, I think, here's a very talented man and a very spiritual man. And a man who's constantly sort of questioning, *Why are we here?* Why are we doing things and how do we treat each other and all that? AND the most neurotic, self-absorbed person. You know, obviously, since we used to always say "Galarry . . ." "Galarry" was the character because it was Garry. The idea that he's examining himself through that character. It's a brilliant form of therapy.

CONAN O'BRIEN I can tell you what it got wrong—which always bugged me—was, how many writers were there? You really got the impression that, okay, he's on every night, and there's two writers that I see. They never seem to be working. Rehearsal is always him like wearing a cowboy hat but very lackadaisical. There's no sense of urgency. That used to piss me off, because I would say, "No no no, you have a gun in your mouth from the time you walk in the front door till the time the show is over." But of course what it got right was the ego there, how neurotic it is. How needy you are. Larry's obsession with *How am I being perceived? How did that go over? What's going on, how is this going?* That is all right on. That is all exactly what it's like.

JUDD It always felt to me like he was ashamed of the Larry Sanders part of himself. And he would always say, "The difference between me and Larry Sanders is Larry Sanders couldn't write *The Larry Sanders Show*."

MAYA FORBES (writer, *The Larry Sanders Show*) What was fun about the tension was that you were writing about it. Whatever was going on, all the tension and the hurt feelings or the neediness, all of the personality that was being exposed by that bunker mentality, was stuff you were then writing about for the show. So I think, for me, it was exciting because it was my first job and I was seeing such a rich crazy landscape that we were then also writing about, this crazy workplace where everyone is scared of Larry and trying to please Larry. It was amazing to be able to have that mirror.

1998

> Richard Day
> My hunch is
> that anyone
> who has me
> confused in any
> ~~way~~ on any
> level with
> Larry Sanders can't
> write the show.

PETER TOLAN The oral history of *Sanders* was littered with the names of writers that he would mention to you later in sort of an offhand way, sometimes as the butt of a joke or just a comic reference. His disappointment was pretty complete. It was very difficult, because that person then was deadweight. He just didn't trust them and they were there.

1998

> proud. Acting
> nominations.
> which means
> that I'm
> acting a part.

"Everybody Has a Curtain": *The Larry Sanders Show*

JUDD I always felt like Garry was such a good writer that it was impossible to rise to his level and have him be satisfied. For the most part you were going to disappoint him because it was like painting with Picasso and he would go, "Why are you using red?" And there was no way to anticipate exactly what he would like and then it would frustrate him.

"Everybody Has a Curtain": *The Larry Sanders Show*

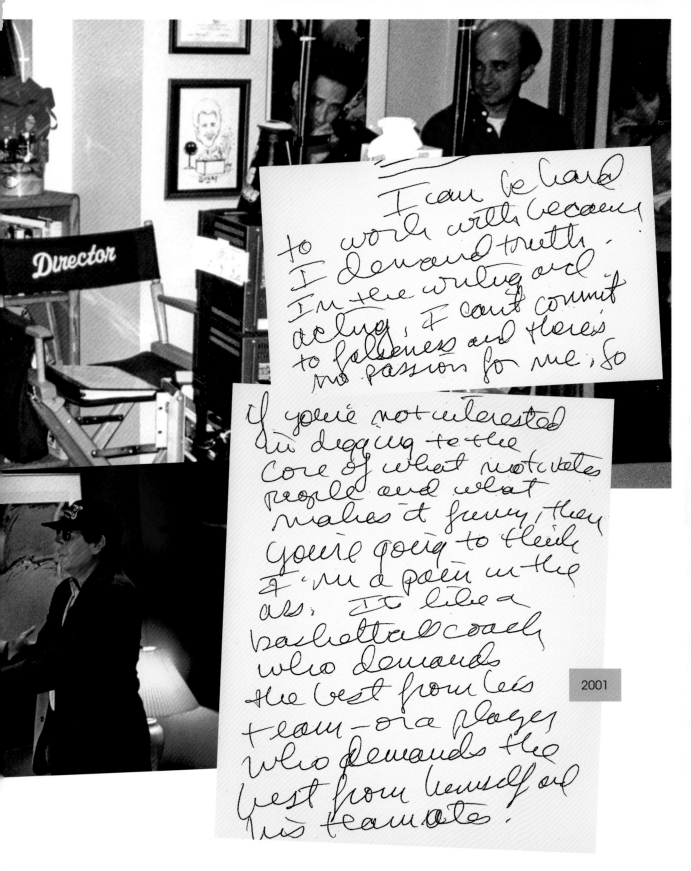

I can be hard to work with because I demand truth. In the writing and acting, I can't commit to falseness and there's no passion for me, so

If you're not interested in digging to the core of what motivates people and what makes it funny, then you're going to think I'm a pain in the ass. It like a basketball coach who demands the best from his team — or a player who demands the best from himself and his teammates.

2001

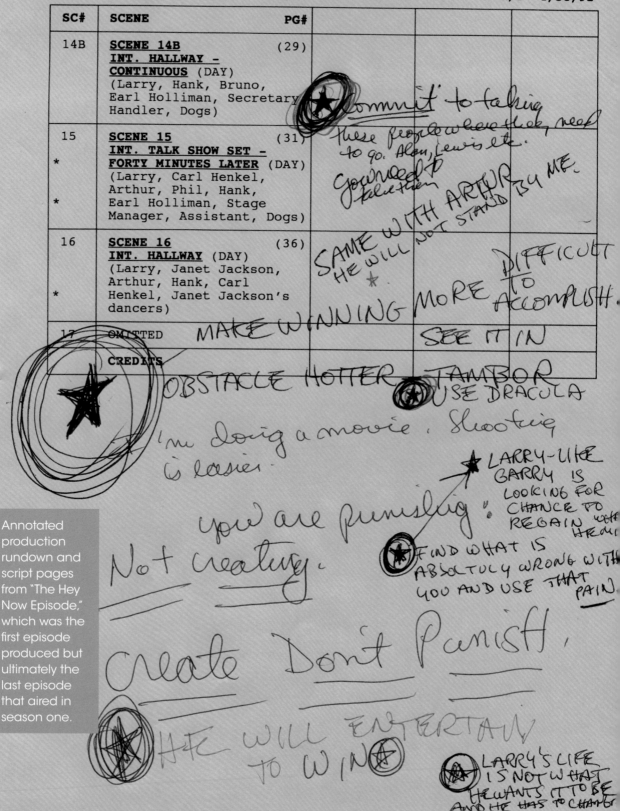

SC#	SCENE	PG#			
14B	**SCENE 14B** **INT. HALLWAY -** **CONTINUOUS** (DAY) (Larry, Hank, Bruno, Earl Holliman, Secretary Handler, Dogs)	(29)			
15 * *	**SCENE 15** **INT. TALK SHOW SET -** **FORTY MINUTES LATER** (DAY) (Larry, Carl Henkel, Arthur, Phil, Hank, Earl Holliman, Stage Manager, Assistant, Dogs)	(31)			
16 *	**SCENE 16** **INT. HALLWAY** (DAY) (Larry, Janet Jackson, Arthur, Hank, Carl Henkel, Janet Jackson's dancers)	(36)			
17	OMITTED				
	CREDITS				

commit to taking these people where they need to go. Alan, Lewis etc. you need television

SAME WITH ARTHUR HE WILL NOT STAND BY ME.

MAKE WINNING MORE DIFFICULT TO ACCOMPLISH.

SEE IT IN

OBSTACLE HOTTER TAMBOR USE DRACULA

I'm doing a movie. Shooting is easier.

you are punishing. Not creating.

★ LARRY-LIKE BARRY IS LOOKING FOR CHANCE TO REGAIN HIS CREDI

FIND WHAT IS ABSOLUTELY WRONG WITH YOU AND USE THAT PAIN.

create Don't Punish.

HE WILL ENTERTAIN TO WIN

LARRY'S LIFE IS NOT WHAT HE WANTS IT TO BE AND HE HAS TO CHANGE

Annotated production rundown and script pages from "The Hey Now Episode," which was the first episode produced but ultimately the last episode that aired in season one.

3   CONTINUED: 3

                    ARTHUR
          Earl Holliman who's got
          another new TV series, and an
          author. And... don't panic.
          Dana Carvey dropped out, but
          I'm working on a third guest
          now.

                    LARRY
          Who's Arsenio got tomorrow
          night?

                    ARTHUR
          He's got Schwarzenegger and
          Dana Carvey.
                    (off Larry's look)
          I'm kidding. All he's got is
          Dudley Moore. The network is
          pushing Donna Mills.

                    LARRY
          Donna Mills? I'd like to push
          her off a fucking bridge. For
          God's sake, even "KISS" is
          working without makeup now.

Hank passes by with a young, attractive woman and RAY
COMBS.

                    HANK
          Hi Arthur. Hey Larry, you
          know my friend Ray, the host
          of "Family Feud?"

                    LARRY
          Ray.

                    RAY
          Yeah, hi Larry. We're on our
          way to the Smokehouse. You
          want to go?

                    HANK
          We're gonna have a couple
          beerskis.

                    LARRY
          No, as much as I like
          beerskis... The survey says
          no.

                                              (CONTINUED)

Handwritten annotations:

Top left: Commit to having other person feel it. * Not the audience. They don't desire to feel it — the person does.

Left margin: Commit to having someone — see this emotion

had been working without makeup

Left lower: Let loose of showing people you're angry. Don't cover anger.

Near Larry/Hank: physical react can. To Hank. * Hank to know he regrets me.

Top right: you're not doing your job!

Right: Humor's not going to save you. Or I wish you didn't jolo this way

Right middle: See this Artie

Center: I want Hank to know what I feel!! *

Right: Cover that I was talking about Hank

Right: Talk to me so I don't have to talk to Hank

Right: See how charming I can be Hank. I still don't have to talk to him

Bottom right: If I don't keep this up I'll have to confront Hank.

10   CONTINUED: (2)   10

(handwritten: A CHANGE) (NURTURING) (I DO AN this job) (Become the BOSS)

                    LARRY
          Hank, could we talk for a
          moment?

(handwritten left: Now I'm ready to go)

                    HANK
          Sure.

(handwritten: FIGHT TO WIN) (I LOVE HANK N) (NOT COMING INTO) (HAVE AN ARGUMENT)

          They walk into:

                                        CUT TO:

(handwritten right: So as not to let anyone in the office know there's a problem like way you said to Dennis: "Can I ask you somethin in bathroom" Like Dennis in Bathroom if you don't know when to stop")

11   INT. LARRY'S OFFICE - CONTINUOUS

(handwritten left: SUBST LINDA Jealousy)

          Larry and Hank enter.

                    LARRY
          Close the door.

          Hank closes the door. Larry sits.

(handwritten: Energy of I'm the BOSS)

                    LARRY (CONT'D)
          Why do you say "Hey Now!"?

                    HANK
          What do you mean?

(handwritten: DON'T STAY WITH ANGER:) (EDUCATE HIM) (THAT'S A LOSER)

(handwritten left: I want you to see that I feel you are ridiculous) (Do you get that you are a clown?)

                    LARRY
          Hank, you know, I guess I've
          never brought it up before,
          but this "Hey Now!" thing is
          just an affectation, isn't it?
          I mean, did you used to say it
          in your personal life? I
          can't believe that when you
          were a kid you said "Hey Now!"
          Did you?

(handwritten right: I know this is true It an affected hook)

                    HANK
          I probably didn't but I said
          "Hey" and I said "Now" at
          different times but never put
          them together until later in
          life. So in that sense, it's
          part of my personality.

(handwritten: MY GOAL'S MORE IMPORTANT TO WIN THIS MAN'S LOVE.)

(handwritten left: STOP THE FRUSTRATION AND ANGER IT WON'T HELP YOU.)

                    LARRY
          Look, this is not easy for me,
          but would you mind not doing
          it on the show anymore
          because, frankly...

(handwritten: I can't stand to go on Like this co-ar wonderful tea)

(handwritten right: Change He is another way to show you how much this bother you)

                                        (CONTINUED)

(handwritten bottom: I'm here to create Hank as my friend not to punish him)

SCOTT THOMPSON ("BRIAN")

I think he saw me on *Conan*. Nobody was openly gay back then, and I think he was just kind of astounded that I was kind of free, I guess. Coming into the show, Garry wanted me to be the assistant to Hank. I thought, "Well, wouldn't it be interesting if the character was actually not a really flamboyant guy, and that he was the only person in the office that actually liked Hank. And became devoted to him." And I remember Garry going, "We can work with that." And then I said, "I want one thing. I want him to be Canadian." I said, "I think that's quite radical. There's never been an openly Canadian character."

SCOTT My second week on *Larry Sanders*, my brother committed suicide. I was in complete shock, and I remember my boyfriend taking me to the *Sanders* set. I was crying and I was a mess. And Garry took me into his office and I just wept like a baby and he talked to me all through it. He told me about his brother, and he told me what happened to him, and how he had this sadness inside of him and he just—and I heard that he never spoke about his brother but he did to me. I don't really remember much of the details, I just remember that it gave me peace. It helped me because he said I can relate, I know what you're going through.

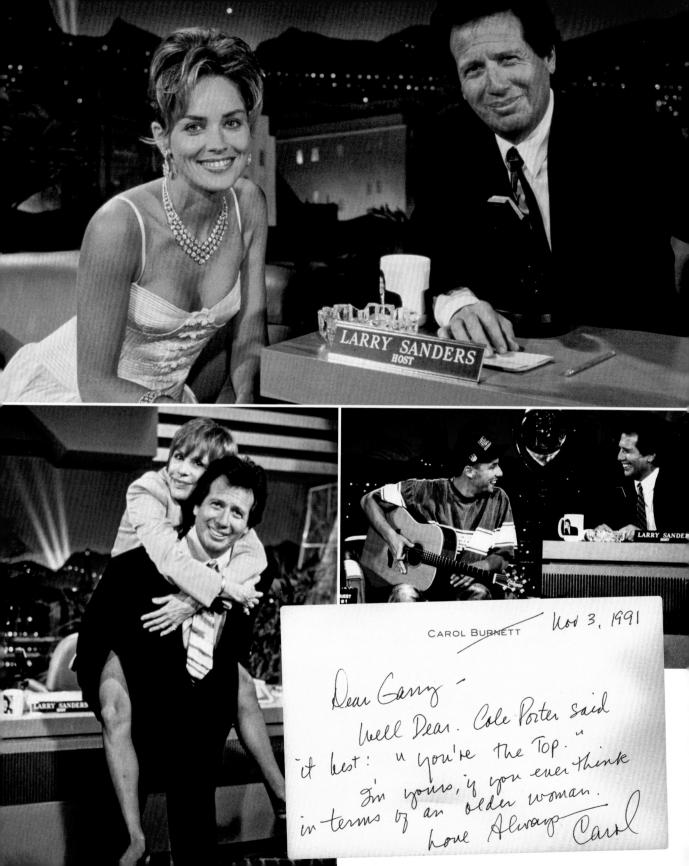

CAROL BURNETT   Nov 3, 1991

Dear Garry -
      Well Dear. Cole Porter said
it best: " you're the Top. "
         I'm yours, if you ever think
in terms of an older woman.
                  Love Always,
                              Carol

JUDD I got in a big fight with Garry about the "My Name Is Asher Kingsley" episode. Because I said, "You can't do an episode about Hank being Jewish without talking about Larry being Jewish." And he said, "Larry isn't Jewish." And I started laughing, and he got really mad at me. He was like, "We've never said he's Jewish. He has a Christmas tree." I'm like, "I had a Christmas tree as a kid, that doesn't mean anything." I go, "Of course he's Jewish." I go, "You're the Jewiest-looking guy in the world." And he looked at me—he was so mad. But then what he did is he turned it into a joke, which was that Larry always denies he's Jewish, and then someone says to Rip, "What religion is Larry?" and he goes, "He's a talk show host." And Ben Stiller screams at Garry, "You self-hating Jew!" in another episode, and Larry says, "You think I'm Jewish?"

                           HANK
          You're overreacting.

                           ARTHUR
          Okay. Let's put it this way. If
          you have an office full of people
          discussing religion, it separates
          them. Take our little group. Phil
          is a Buddhist.

                           HANK
          I didn't know that.

                           ARTHUR
          Exactly my point. Beverly is a
          Christian. And Paula is an
          atheist. I myself am a Democrat.
          But we all join hands to put this
          show together every night. And I
          don't want you to fuck that up.

                           HANK
          What religion is Larry?

                           ARTHUR
          Larry is a talk show host. Shalom,
          baby.

                                        CUT TO:

4   INT. WRITERS ROOM - A LITTLE LATER (DAY 1)   4*

      Phil sits at the table reading the morning paper. Hank
      enters.

                           HANK
          Good morning.

                           PHIL
          Good morning, Hank.

                           HANK
          Listen, I had a question about that
          sketch you wrote about the one size
          fits all condom.

                           PHIL
          What about it?

                                        (CONTINUED)

JUDD On a normal show, you might say, "Okay, we're gonna write ten episodes before the season starts." But we never even knew what celebrities would be on the show. And so there was no way to get ahead: "Warren Beatty just canceled and we have an offer out to Jeff Goldblum."

JEFF GOLDBLUM I think I thought to myself sometimes, *Geez, how can they really carry on doing any more talk shows like this now? This is not just a satire, it's an X-ray. Isn't this the last talk show?*

Dec 22

I haven't been so angry in years. Two days ago, I walked off the set and did not complete shooting the season. All I asked was when I say that I can't do any more hate at night after a full day of working, don't push me. It was pushed over my brink

While filming the season 5 episode "The Roast," a particularly long and contentious night of shooting led to Garry walking off the set—an action that would later be used against him.

All I ask is don't push
me over my brink — over
the edge. And they can't
help themselves... all for
one shitty 3 minute monolog.
This is why people like
me end up putting walls
around themselves and
others think they are
becoming assholes. What
the truth is, is that
they cause it. If Buddha
is meditating and someone
shakes him, and he says,
"please do not shake me,
shake yourself," and the
person keeps shaking until
Buddha hits him. Then
the person will say, "Ah
you don't want to be shaken"
then the Buddha would
go back to his meditation

all of them are just unaware

people, not knowing what to do. The Buddha way is too embrace them. I can only turn to God: to myself.

If one of them said to me, "please don't shake me," I wouldn't. If someone said to me, "I can't do anymore tonight," I'd say fine, lets stop. It is destructive to push. But they don't know. They can't empathize with another persons feelings — especially mine, at any place. Did I expect them too? Yes — at least just the part about not pushing me over the edge — to join me and hear me and support me when I say (or they see) that I'm done. But they all just stare like a bunch of impotent morons. I'll never forget the look on everyone's face as I walked off: "What wrong ??!?"

Here are the key phrases I gave them to know when I'm done:

1) I'm done.
2) We're at that place...
3) I can't
4) I don't think so.
5) No.
6) (Look at my face)

The words mean nothing. They are not me and do not understand what I understand. They become abusive and self-destructive. All they have to do is listen to me.

MAYA FORBES You have a table read on Monday. And then Thursday, Friday, you're shooting the entire show except for the talk show element, which you were doing every three weeks with a live audience. When I talk to people now and they're shooting a half hour, they're shooting in what, five or six days? Obviously we had a very contained set. It was crazy. We didn't know, but I think that the pressure of that was causing everyone to have a lot of friction. People would have a lot of friction. It was really hard to keep it at the standard that Garry wanted, and he wasn't making it easier. It was like obliterating your life.

BRUCE GRAYSON I look back at those years—even though it's so fun to listen to people reminisce about *Sanders,* and the crew and everybody was having so much fun—and Garry was just in this terrible, terrible place. But everybody knew there was brilliance happening every week. Every week we'd read through the scripts and go, "Oh, fuck, this is gonna be great."

What show does have good working conditions?

1998

1994

When you work on project, you commit to fixing everything that is wrong. You don't quit.
I'm in this relationship

JUDD He wasn't happy in the beginning of the final season, and he said, "Would you co-run the show with Adam Resnick?" And I said, "Garry, I really don't want you to hate me. I'm really nervous. I value our friendship before the show. So I'll do it, but you can't hate me. I'm going to try really hard." And we came up with this system where after table reads, you know, we would do notes with the staff and rewrite all night, but I tried to get him to do as much of the work on his own as possible. And I said, "Garry, let's make it fun. We'll go in your office. We can do this fast and let's have fun." And we did. We would have fun rewriting it. But it really took looking him in the eye and going, "Don't hate me, Garry. I'm trying."

"Everybody Has a Curtain": *The Larry Sanders Show*

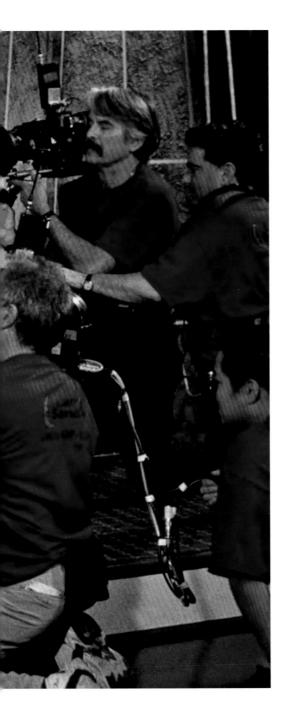

PENNY JOHNSON When he started working on that final season, Garry worked so hard that he diminished in size, even. He got smaller. He would have his meals prepared, and I never saw him eating anymore. He was really working hard. And so I don't know how long he could have kept that up.

PETER TOLAN I would always fight with him and say, "You know, it's a show about backstage at a talk show." About showing that. He loved to do the talk show part of it. So the initial cuts on episodes, you'd be going, "There's eight minutes of the talk show!" It's only like twenty-eight minutes of show. I mean, my God. It was a way for him to sort of get what he wanted, really. In his own terms he sort of got to do a talk show.

GARRY I used stories that happened to me on *The Tonight Show*. Stories that happened to me on all talk shows. Stories that happened on all the shows that I worked on. Other writers used stories from their shows. It became diluted enough that you would often forget who did what to whom. But they were all based in some fact.

Garry accepting an Emmy
for Outstanding Writing for
a Comedy Series.

JAY LENO I think he really got it exactly right. I would watch movies where people play comedians, even as great an actor as Dustin Hoffman, I never quite bought him as Lenny Bruce, because actors, when they play a comedian, they're watching themselves play the comedian. Comedians just give it up, they really don't care what they look like or how stupid they look or whatever. They give it all. And they don't want to see their portrayal because they might change something because it worked. Whenever I see actors play comedians they're always very introspective, just something doesn't ring true about it. But that's what was great about Garry. He was a real comic.

JEFFREY TAMBOR Garry and I had a little set-to once. We got really mad at each other, and I think I went up to him and I said something about "I'm tired of sucking hind tit." I remember saying that phrase and it was like a Hank moment. And going, *Why did that come out of my mouth? I don't even believe that.* And we had a big fight, and I was going through something and so we both slept on it, but we had a scene the next day, and we were both really sorry. And I remember we were about to shoot, and we both said, "Let's not make up yet. Let's bring that into the scene. That was us."

SARAH SILVERMAN Every element of it was so important to him and yet he was oddly not precious. The scripts were so brilliant and he would still say, "Say whatever you want. All that's important is that you get the spirit of this scene across, I don't care what words you use, I don't care if you say any of these lines."

GARRY Some people mistakenly think that's a dark show about people trying to get what they want. No. It is a show about people trying to get love, and that shit gets in the way. They're trying to figure out, with a little lack of awareness, how to get past that shit to get to the love.

LARRY'S LAWSUITS

While *The Larry Sanders Show* was a career high point for Garry, the period also brought him low with a pair of lawsuits from two of the closest people in his life: fiancée Linda Doucett and manager Brad Grey. Doucett had been in a relationship with Garry for seven years and had played Hank's assistant Darlene for three years when she and Garry broke up and she was unceremoniously fired from the show.

LINDA DOUCETT We journaled. We had therapists. We worked so hard on ourselves. Everything was about consciousness and enlightenment and laughter. Which is what we did all the time. We were neurotic and we were incredibly spiritual and searching for our higher selves. That's how we were able to be together. He used to say my biological clock was on snooze alarm. So we were good together and we manifested a lot of good stuff. But because I wanted to become a mother, therapy increased. We had teams. He had a therapist, I had a therapist, we had couples therapy.

My relationship with Linda has reached a critical point. I can't imagine it ending — but I want to be happy in life.

1993

ALAN ZWEIBEL When Linda came around, I thought she was really good for Garry. In her own way, she knew how to handle him. That said, Garry still had his old demons. What Garry didn't like to feel was trapped. I think Garry always needed the option to go here or go there. When he and Linda got engaged, Robin, my wife, asks, "Have you picked a date yet for your wedding?" He was building the house in Brentwood at the time, and Linda says something along the lines of, "No, Garry wants to wait until the house has finished being built, so we can move in together as husband and wife." Well, it was not hard to predict what came next. Every time we'd drive by the house, I'd say, "Robin, wasn't the chimney over there last week? *(Pointing)* It was *there*. Didn't that used to be a two-car garage?" He didn't want this house to be finished being built. Because the longer it was under construction, the longer he didn't have to make that commitment.

LINDA The show became art imitating life. A lot of our situations and things came into play. When you're starring, you're showrunning, you're writing, you're parodying the dark side of your own personal life—it's a lot. So it became very difficult, because we were having a human spiritual experience, and I wanted to become more of a mother. So it's like our paths changed. I think the thought of losing a child, to him . . . He lost a brother. And his mother, you know, I think went a little crazy because of that. So, you know, children became an issue for Garry. When you have the cystic fibrosis illness in your family, you have a chance of carrying that gene. I think it was more about: If he loved a child so much, what if the child died like his brother died?

JUDD Well, that's complicated. He doesn't want to have children. You do. But now you're also working on the television show together, so you're tied together at work.

LINDA (*Nodding*) Work. And then, after Garry and I broke up, my agent called and said I was fired. But you have to understand that there were so many people advising him now, that the human personal experience is now removed. It's business.

JUDD It seemed like Garry didn't understand that when you guys broke up, that you're not allowed to fire your ex-fiancée from her show.

LINDA You know, it's amazing how we started off mocking the industry and then we fell prey to it.

Why can't I commit? Give to Linda? Give what?

Not long after the split with Doucett, Garry lost another close relationship in a cloud of legal acrimony—although this time he was the aggrieved party. In 1998, Garry filed a $100 million civil suit against his former agent and manager Brad Grey, alleging Grey had been taking advantage of their professional relationship for his own personal gain. Grey then responded with a countersuit. While they would eventually reach a settlement that Garry was satisfied with, the episode took a personal toll on his trust and well-being.

"Everybody Has a Curtain": *The Larry Sanders Show*

Garry and Brad in earlier days.

"I can't believe
you think your
agent is your
friend."
—Artie to Larry

I didn't know
I needed a lawyer.

When I found
he had taken
commissions. Advised me
not to get a lawyer.

This is not
about a personal
relationship
This is a business
dispute

He took money
without telling

me. When I
asked ~~I couldn't~~

couldn't get
explanation of
of these deals and
contracts

3/ Look at those
contract to see
how I and my show
was used by my
personal manager
to enrich himself.

1998

Jan. 21

I filed a lawsuit
against Brad Grey.
Continue to focus
on my work and the
way.

BOB SAGET They started together. And they rose together. Brad had a few clients— I was the first, Garry was the second. I was at The Comedy Store in Westwood and Brad Grey brought his boss and partner in management, Harvey Weinstein, to come see Garry perform. And I went up, but it was really Garry's night, to see if he wanted to sign with my management, because I was getting gigs opening for Kenny Loggins and Frankie Valli and the Four Seasons, and Garry wanted that. He wanted to open for people. And Brad was like, "I'll get you those gigs." And so [Garry] started doing a lot of stand-up. And Garry stayed with Brad. And they did great things together, they really did. And it's real unfortunate that that happened.

It's about standing up for what's right and having the courage to defend the truth.

DAVE COULIER It was like you worked for Brad. It was as if the roles were reversed. Brad became so connected within the industry, and he was so smart, and had such a keen eye for the business of comedy, that it seemed like you were working for Brad. It was an amazing thing to see; as much as a legend Bernie Brillstein was, Brad started to even surpass Bernie. So it was really interesting to kinda sit back and watch this transformation.

GAVIN DE BECKER (Garry's friend/ author) The lawyer that Garry had engaged asked Brad's group, "Hey, can we see these contracts, whatever it is that Garry signed?" And nothing came back and nothing came back and nothing came back; eventually the lawyer came to Garry and said, "I cannot get these contracts." And so Garry went and asked, and the general response from Brad was "You don't want to ask this question." Sort of an organized-crime response. He just couldn't get his own contracts. And then, as you do get them, piece by piece, they look pretty unfair. You've got Brad earning more money on the show than Garry's earning on the show, things like that.

BILL ISAACSON (Garry's friend and lawyer) When Garry was starting in stand-up, Brad Grey was representing him and helping him get gigs and they were very close friends. And as Garry succeeded, so did Brad. Then Brad became 50 percent owner of *Larry Sanders Show*. At the same time, he's the manager, so he receives commissions, and he's the producer, so he gets producer fees. And he began to use his reputation that he was getting from that to spin off into other shows and then to do production deals. I don't think it actually occurred to people that your business manager should not take half of your show. And, all of a sudden, the writers from *Larry Sanders* were being offered deals at other shows. So, you're sitting there saying, "My producer and my co-owner is taking away our talent." That really upset Garry. Because anything that made the job more difficult or took creative people that he wanted to work with away from him was taking away from *Larry Sanders Show*. But it just came down to: Your manager is taking a commission to represent your interests and is not supposed to be representing his interests. This person had a duty of loyalty.

November 17, 1997

BY FACSIMILE (310-553-0687)

Bertram Fields, Esq.
Greenberg, Glusker, Fields, Claman & Machtinger
1900 Avenue of the Stars #2000
Los Angeles, CA 90067

RE: **Garry Shandling**

Dear Bert:

Thanks for yours of November 9, 1997. In keeping with your suggestion, in behalf of Mr. Shandling I am hereby requesting that Brillstein-Grey provide all financial documents, records, contracts, etc. in connection with the above-entitled television series for review by Mr. Shandling, his accountants and other representatives. Please advise the earliest date on which the aforesaid may be delivered to this office.

Best regards.

Sincerely,

Barry L. Hirsch

BLH:pr

cc: Mr. Garry Shandling
      Mr. Warren Grant

May 26

Your attitude pertaining to the law suit must be and will be : "Bring it on. None of this bothers me. None of this bothers me. Bring it on. Press stories? None of it bothers me. I've never felt better.

1998

"Everybody Has a Curtain": *The Larry Sanders Show*

Hey, now! Ex-manager turns tables on Garry

By JOSEF ADALIAN

Garry Shandling is now being sued by the former manager whom he sued last month.

THE war between Garry Shandling and his ex-manager just took another bizarre turn.

In a scene straight out of "The Larry Sanders Show," Hollywood power broker Brad Grey — who, until last November, was Shandling's friend, manager and business partner — yesterday sued the neurotic comic for $10 million. Grey is claiming Shandling's "erratic and destructive" behavior ruined their partnership and cost Grey millions in potential profits.

The suit, filed in Los Angeles Superior Court, is a response to the $100 million legal action Shandling filed against Grey in January. Shandling claimed his star power helped Grey and partner Bernie Brillstein build up their TV produc-

tion company, Brillstein-Grey Enterprises, which produces Shandling's HBO series, "The Larry Sanders Show." As a result, Shandling says he's entitled to 50 percent of Brillstein-Grey's television profits.

"It's an unpleasant circumstance, but we intend to prevail," Grey told The Post.

Grey's attorney, Bert Fields told The Post that Shandling's version of events is "demonstrable hogwash."

Grey's countersuit is filled with juicy accusations against Shandling, including charges that Shandling:

■ "Mistreated numerous writers and staff, to the point where several . . . found working with Shandling intolerable and left the show."

■ "Arbitrarily fired other talented staff members and then denigrated their abilities."

■ "Caused costly and repeated production delays by his self-destructive conduct."

■ "Suddenly quit the show in 1996, thereby leaving production incomplete." (Shandling later returned. The series begins its final season later this month.)

Shandling's attorneys issued a statement charging Grey with "mudslinging" and seeking to "enrich himself at Mr. Shandling's expense."

Through a spokesman, Shandling said he was "warned that Brad Grey was going to smear me, so I'm not surprised. I'm relieved. I thought he was going to say I wasn't funny."

I suppose you knew about this

I can't wait to get into court. 12 people is my best-size audience

LINDA DOUCETT The lawsuit brought us back into contact. What happened was that the three people that were relevant in that lawsuit were the three people that were together during that whole time, which was Garry, me, and Brad. It was Brad and Garry both trying to sway me to go their direction. So it was even more surreal. Because I had to chew my arm to get out and survive; now I'm back in it. And which way and how and who.

GAVIN DE BECKER What I always felt Garry needed was Artie. Garry needed an Artie, and he didn't have that. And he had, instead, Brad Grey.

Top: A newspaper article Garry's mom sent him, on which she had written, "I suppose you knew about this."

Hey, Now!

FEUDS Garry Shandling shocks Hollywood with his $100 million suit against former manager Brad Grey. **by Joe Flint**

GARRY SHANDLING HAS MADE IT OFFI-cial: The upcoming season of his critically acclaimed HBO series, *The Larry Sanders Show*, will be the last. He says he's got a terrific idea for a finale, although it will be hard to top this real-life scenario: Garry becomes convinced that his high-powered manager has been robbing him blind and sues him for millions. Said manager questions the sanity of his longtime client, as does much of Hollywood.

It's a plot so suited to *Larry Sanders*—a show that brilliantly spoofs a tortured, paranoid late-night host—that much of the industry was waiting for the punchline. But in the end, it was no laughing matter. In a feud that could make the Jeffrey Katzenberg–Michael Eisner contretemps look like a love tap, Shandling filed a $100 million lawsuit against his manager, Brad Grey, as well as Grey's management and production company, Brillstein-Grey Enterprises.

Shandling, 48, is claiming that Grey abused his trust and reaped millions from their association. Specifically, the comic wants a cut of what Brillstein-Grey made from a $100 million development deal with ABC and the firm's $90 million sale of half its production arm to Universal Studios. Those deals, Shandling's suit alleges, would not have happened "without assurance of [his] exclusive involvement in Grey's ventures."

Ted Harbert would beg to differ. The former ABC Entertainment chairman insists that the Alphabet deal had almost nothing to do with Shandling; he is just one in a "very extensive and appealing list of clients," says Harbert. "The network made the deal to be in business with Brillstein-Grey Enterprises."

Still, if nothing else, the suit sheds light on a growing industry concern: managers who do double duty as producers—as Grey does as an executive producer on *Larry Sanders*. It's a confusing *and* fine line to walk, given the attendant job descriptions: Managers must determine what's best for their clients; a producer's priorities should be the show and the studio producing it. Shandling is accusing Grey of stepping over that line by putting his own interests ahead of Shandling's. "Other Brillstein-Grey clients recognize that Brad negotiates *with* them, not *for* them. That is what our case is about," says Shandling's attorney, Jonathan D. Schiller.

Making the situation even stickier, Shandling and Grey were close friends for 18 years—that is, until Grey dumped Shandling as a client last November. To hear Grey's camp tell it, Shandling's neurotic behavior—both on and off the set—finally went too far. "Garry became Larry Sanders," says a longtime colleague of Shandling. "He's been abusive toward Brad and others on the show." Case in point: In January, Shandling's latest producer, Craig Zisk, quit in frustration, only to be persuaded by Grey to return to the show.

Shandling—who owns a 50 percent stake in his HBO series and earns nearly $500,000 per episode—*has* had a revolving door of writers and producers since the show's 1992 launch, many of whom have gone on to helm their own sitcoms, including *NewsRadio*'s Paul Simms and *Just Shoot Me*'s Steven Levitan. Shandling is charging not only that Grey diverted talent from *Larry Sanders* to other Brillstein-Grey-produced sitcoms but that he deserves a piece of those careers. "Throughout his career, Grey...relied on Shandling to identify and develop comic talents, talents who helped establish Grey's...success," says Schiller.

Grey, 40, is not talking beyond a diplomatic statement released through his office. Grey's partner, Bernie Brillstein, however, minced no words in his official comment: "We have made millions of dollars *for* him. I know that Garry has been fond of Brad for years, but I never knew he felt entitled to community property. [His] claims are delusional." Grey's attorney, Bert Fields, seconds that: "You drive guys off your series and they go work for other series and then you say you own that series. The suit is sheer lunacy."

It's been particularly hard for friends of both Shandling and Grey, many of whom refuse to take sides. But those who have gone public tend to support Grey. "Brad has been my manager and friend for over 20 years. [He's] a person of extraordinary honor and integrity," says Bob Saget, who introduced Shandling to Grey. "For these reasons," he quipped, "I feel I should get 100 percent of his business, and I also have my eye on one of his cars."

The truth will, no doubt, emerge as the specifics of the case are revealed in court. Shandling will deliver his verdict sooner: In an episode rumored to be in the works, Larry Sanders will fire his manager. ∎

Loose Lips sink ship. *

Brad's PR * Machine is working overtime to detract from the facts of the case. The litigatory

I'm thinking about creative projects.

He's trying to win it in court of public opinion. Court. madamit.

Limit the amount that you read about the case. Keep focused on the work. Stay creative. Do not make this the most important thing. Stay out of it. If it goes well it goes well... ~~and~~ if it goes bad, it goes bad

If you discover truth is thru this then it is a victory. You must do this better than anyone ever thought you could.

This man had conflicts, this man attempted lies and character assassanton.

It not about money. It about standing up for yourself.

BRUCE GRAYSON Betrayal became a big component in Garry's life. If there was an element of betrayal or dishonesty after Brad, a lot of people were dropped, a lot of friendships were just dropped.

GARRY There are people who seek truth and there are people who manipulate truth for their own good. That's the conflict in life. That's the conflict in Hollywood. That's the conflict that's depicted on this show. It's a wonderful, sad reality. I'd rather watch it on TV than live it.

Shandling suit settled

By DAVID K. LI

LOS ANGELES — Comedian Garry Shandling and mega-producer Brad Grey quietly settled the comic's $100 million lawsuit yesterday, heading off a trial that threatened to rock Hollywood.

Lawyers on both sides did not return phone calls seeking comment.

Grey, a partner in the high-power management firm Brillstein-Grey, was Shandling's manager for 18 years, and directed the comedian to stardom in Fox's "It's the Garry Shandling Show" and the wildly popular HBO sitcom "The Larry Sanders Show."

Brillstein-Grey co-owned and produced "Sanders," which is no longer on the air. Shandling accused Grey of triple-dipping — by taking a manager's cut, pay as the show's producer and a piece of the "Sanders" show's profits.

Garry Shandling.

The question, still unsettled because there was no trial, is whether a manager can also profit as the client's producer without having a conflict of interest. More and more Hollywood managers are expanding their roles and producing shows for their clients.

A statement from Shandling's publicist yesterday suggested that the comedian scored some profits from Brillstein-Grey.

"In the settlement, each of the parties acquired from the other certain interests in various television programs," according to Shandling's statement.

"Mr. Shandling and I are very pleased that an amicable settlement has been achieved without the necessity of a trial," Shandling's lawyer David Boies said, according to the release.

Jury selection was set to start yesterday in Los Angeles, but the two sides jointly filed for dismissal before the proceedings got underway. Shandling had filed the lawsuit in January 1998.

I did the right thing, I stood up for myself — it wasn't about revenge

"Everybody Has a Curtain": *The Larry Sanders Show*

DAVID DUCHOVNY He was obsessed with that relationship having dissolved. I think he was heartbroken on top of it all. And it reminded me of a marriage; it reminded me of a love affair that somebody is still in, but out of at the same time.

ANITA BUSCH (journalist) What happened affected him on a cellular level. We often talked about that. On a cellular level it hurt him physically, it hurt him mentally, it hurt his confidence, it hurt him spiritually.

JUDD As a result of Garry's lawsuit, it seems to have changed the business a bit.

GAVIN DE BECKER Yes, that's true. I mean, people certainly recognized that you cannot be somebody's manager and be the studio all at the same time. And that's really what the legacy of that case is.

BOB SAGET When I signed with Brad, when he was twenty and I was twenty-two, I knew without a question of a doubt that he was going to rise to the top of whatever he wanted to do. Brad was not a bad person. Brad was a businessman and he loved Garry. And he was one of the most giving people for my family and for my life that will ever be in my life. But, when Garry came after him with all guns blazing, I think he felt betrayed because, if you sue someone for $100 million, you're saying that you want to destroy that person. Or at least his reputation. I had two friends that I loved who were basically going through a very upsetting divorce. And I couldn't not be friends with Brad anymore, but I also couldn't not be friends with Garry anymore. But that's what Garry wanted.

JUDD Well, what did he think was happening?

BOB I think he felt I chose a side, when I wanted to talk to him because I had none of those grievances nor understanding. And Brad and his family and his kids are like my kids, and I love them. And so I can't have my god-child anymore? You know? It's . . . "I need to talk to you about this, Garry."

JUDD Why did Garry think you were on Brad's side?

BOB I made one joke. Someone said, "Are you gonna sue Brad?" And I said, "No, but I have my eye on one of his cars." So, it was an innocuous joke.

JUDD What do you think Garry expected from you in that moment? What do you think Garry thinks was—

BOB That's what I don't know.

JUDD 'Cause it seems like Garry wasn't able to shut off his hurt enough to go, *Oh, what would I do in their situation?*

BOB As hurt as he was, I was pretty fucking hurt. So I just kept trying to call Garry to say, "I wanna talk to you." And he didn't want to.

"Everybody Has a Curtain": *The Larry Sanders Show*

DAVID BOIES (in his book *Courting Justice: From NY Yankees v. Major League Baseball to Bush v. Gore, 1997–2000*) From the beginning of our negotiations [with Bert Fields] that evening, I had made clear that any settlement would have to include a substantial cash payment. Bert had initially not agreed, but he had not disagreed either. Once we reached a tentative understanding that Grey would return his interests in both *The Larry Sanders Show* and *It's Garry Shandling's Show,* we turned to the subject of what the guaranteed cash payment would be. It was this issue that consumed most of the several hours we spent together that evening and most of Bert's wine. During the discussion, Bert repeatedly

argued that Grey was entitled to some ownership interest in *The Larry Sanders Show* and that, as a result, if Shandling got back Grey's remaining 25 percent of that show's profits, along with Grey's percentage of Shandling's earlier show, that was enough. I argued that Grey's exposure on the ABC and MCA deals alone justified an eight-figure payment. Eventually we reached agreement on an amount we both considered reasonable.

BILL ISAACSON Lawsuit's filed January 1998. The last season of *Larry Sanders* starts in March, which is really about the lawsuit. It's him reacting to the whole issue of conflicts of interest.

LARRY
Oh, for which client?

STEVIE
No, it was for me. It was for
Entertainment Weekly. The fifty most
powerful people in Hollywood under
thirty.

LARRY
Aren't you thirty-two?

STEVIE
Yeah.

LARRY
Congratulations.

STEVIE
Thank you.

LARRY
So did you talk to the network?

STEVIE
Oh, you mean did I kick the shit out of
them and stuff their heads in a toilet
and flush it nineteen times in a row?

LARRY
And?

STEVIE
One year, no bump.

LARRY
How many times did you flush the toilet?

STEVIE
What are you trying to say?

LARRY
What do you mean?

STEVIE
Sounds like you're trying to imply that I
didn't do my best.

Artie approaches and stands just close enough to be able to
hear.

(CONTINUED)

                    LARRY
        This is about Jon Stewart, isn't it?   *ABC*
        They're just using me as some fucking
        negotiating tool.

                    STEVIE
        Larry, are you smoking crack again?

We hear the band kick in and Hank start Larry's intro.

                    LARRY   *Here I go*
        Who represents Jon Stewart, anyway?

                    STEVIE
        I do.

Beat.

                    LARRY
        You do? Since when?

                    STEVIE   *Network meeting*
        Today at lunch.

                    LARRY
        I thought you were at a photo shoot.

                    STEVIE   *Realize in this moment*
        Before that.

                    LARRY
        Isn't that a bit of a conflict, Stevie?   *SUBSTIE*

                    STEVIE
        Not for me. That's what life is:
        conflict.

                    LARRY
        Uh-huh.

                    STEVIE
        It's all about balance. And I think I do
        a pretty good fucking job.

A long silent beat.

                    HANK (O.S.)
        ...[need a whole intro] Larry Sanders!   *I have to go be on television now.*

Arthur holds open the curtain for Larry.

                                            CUT TO:

                                        (CONTINUED)

KEVIN NEALON (comedian) I swear to you, we would be on the phone late at night, after like an hour or two, and he would mention that. "I think my phone's being tapped," because you hear clicking. Garry had that crazy side to him too, a little paranoid and neurotic. And I would just roll my eyes and think, *Well, okay. Not likely, but okay.* He seemed very paranoid about a lot of things at that point. But it did turn out to be true.

GAVIN DE BECKER Anthony Pellicano was a very aggressive, intimidating private investigator who was not reluctant to break the law in terms of wiretapping. And he worked for an attorney named Bert Fields often, who was the attorney that was against Garry in the lawsuit that he brought against Brad Grey. There's a lot of stuff that's not known, because you don't have Pellicano admitting everything. The FBI has established that he was recording Garry's phone calls, but they have not been able to break the electronic data file to get to all of those phone calls, which would have been important proof in the case as well. But ultimately he did get convicted for wiretapping.

BILL ISAACSON [In 2008] Garry testified at a public trial. At that point Pellicano is just proud of himself that he's not squealing on his clients and he's not letting anybody in his hard drive, but he doesn't have any money to pay for a lawyer, so he's representing himself. So the government put Garry on, and Garry told his story.

```
1   Q.    Good morning, sir.  How are you today?

2   A.    Thank you.  Fine.

3   Q.    What do you do for a living?

4   A.    That's a bad sign.  I'm a comedian.

5         THE COURT:  Not today, sir.

6         THE WITNESS:  I understand that.

7         THE COURT:  Thank you.
```

Court transcript from Garry's testimony.

A18 FRIDAY, MARCH 14, 2008   LOS ANGELES TIMES

Pellicano orchestrated smear, comedian testifies

[Pellicano, from Page A1] he describe the negative stories, other than to say that reporters told him they were planted by Pellicano.

But with its famous names and charges of chicanery, Shandling's testimony hinted at what federal authorities have been alleging for years: that Pellicano and others resorted to dirty tricks to sidestep the justice system and give his powerful clients an upper hand in battles inside and

ment's witness list.

In a statement released by his spokesman, Grey said: "I am extremely saddened by Garry's recollection of events dating back more than a decade. His representation is very different than what I remember and what I know to be true."

Grey said his ... ship with Shandling ... when he and his ... company were suc... median and he hir...

being tried on 110 counts of wiretapping, conspiracy, racketeering and other federal charges after a six-year federal investigation into allegations that he illegally investigated targets and bribed sources to gain an edge for clients. Pellicano and his four co-defendants are ... ex-LAPD Sgt. Mark Arne-

Keith Carradine; and former Beverly Hills Police Officer Craig Stevens.

Pellicano will be tried later on separate counts with entertainment attorney Terry Christensen.

Shandling's 45 minutes of serious testimony began lightheartedly when Assistant U.S.

LES TIMES   CALIFORNIA

Pellicano jury hears first A-list testimony

Comedian Garry Shandling says private eye planted negative stories about him after he sued his manager.

By GREG KRIKORIAN
Times Staff Writer

Comedian Garry Shandling offered a somber and sometimes pained account Thursday of a "smear campaign" he said Anthony Pellicano orchestrated against him while the private eye was working for Paramount Pictures executive Brad Grey and entertainment attorney Bert Fields.

The first celebrity witness to testify in the racketeering and wiretap trial of Pellicano and four others, Shandling told federal jury that he became th...

Pellicano Pleads Guilty Midway Through Trial

[Pellicano, from Page B1] agents descended on his office searching for evidence that might link him to a threat made against a Los Angeles Times reporter. The reporter, Anita Busch, was researching the relationship between actor Steven Seagal and a reputed Mafia figure.

Alexander Proctor, a convicted drug dealer, has been charged with leaving a dead fish and a rose on the hood of Busch's car with a sign reading, "Stop." During a secretly recorded conversation with an FBI informant, Proctor allegedly said that Pellicano paid him to carry out the threat on behalf of Seagal. Both Pellicano and Seagal have denied any involvement.

Although Pellicano has not been charged in the threat case, evidence seized during the search o... arrest and set... federal ... legation... gaged i... tapping... promin...

Pelli... skip tr... high sc... during ... auto e... rean be... Los An... key go... up dar... undern... nesses.

Afte... succes... represe... stars ... Elizabe... son, K... anne ... applie... audio ... forcem... countr...

Pellicano Sentenced To 15 Years In Prison

By BROOKS BARNES

LOS ANGELES — Anthony Pellicano, a private investigator whose client list once included many Hollywood stars, was sentenced on Monday to 15 years in prison for his role in an illegal wiretapping enterprise.

The sentence, from Judge Dale S. Fischer of Federal District Court, was in line with what prosecutors had recommended. Mr. Pellicano, 64, already in custody, was found guilty in two different trials earlier this year on 78 charges, including wiretapping, racketeering and wire fraud. He and his two co-defendants were also ordered to pay a fine of $2 million.

A court-appointed attorney for Mr. Pellicano sought leniency, citing in part a financial struggle by his client to provide for an autistic son as a cause for his behavior. "I have taken full and complete responsibility," Mr. Pellicano said in the courtroom, stand-

The investigator had been found guilty of 78 charges.

Hollywood's Pellicano called a 'well-paid thug'

LOS ANGELES — Private investigator Anthony Pellicano was a "well-paid thug" who dug up dirt through wiretaps and other illegal means to benefit his Hollywood A-list clientele, a federal prosecutor told jurors Tuesday.

"Tires get slashed, computers get hacked, houses get broken into," Assistant U.S. Atty. Dan Saunders said in closing arguments. "And of course, people's

phones get wiretapped."

Pellicano, 64, is accused of leading a criminal enterprise that raked in more than $2 million by spying on Hollywood's rich and famous then supplying the dirt to their rivals.

On the stand: Witnesses included comedian Garry Shandling, an alleged victim, comedian Chris Rock and one-time power agent Michael Ovitz.

Jan 23

Last show 19-20 march
Duchovy Modovera
Eric Idle Sean Penn
Sharon Stone
Jeff Goldblume,
Meg Ryan
Drew carrey, ellen,
Seinfeld, Candice,
Johnny
Robotical fraqual
Al gore
Cher
Jim wood
Glen Close
Kevin
Rozlen

march 21 End series
  "   30 End eclity
April 1 — fly to.
Howaii - fiji
Australia

CURTAIN CALL

The Larry Sanders Show was already considered one of television's most groundbreaking comedies when it entered its sixth, and final, season. Garry was determined to go out on a high note, not only for posterity's sake but also to prove that the work could be just as good without Brad Grey's input. The series finale is still considered to be one of the best in the medium, as lovely and bittersweet as any other farewell.

I've been in
Fiji for a week
and have been
editing a couple
of episodes and
I'm reminded
how right it is
to be ending the
show. There is no

other choice. The
writing mistakes
are so evident.
The editing is so
difficult. The difficulty
of here the line
producer not doing
his job.

But, I am
grateful for
the opportunity and
success. It is

a fantastic show
that I'm proud
of. I came to
L.A. dreaming
of doing "something"
in comedy and
I've had two
successful television
series and guest
hosted the Tonite
show. The last

series is called
by some, "the
best on T.V."
I am grateful
for the experience—
I have learned
and been given
success. I can
come to Fiji or
Hawaii anytime
I want. I am
grateful for the
good things that
have happened in
my life. I thank

June 1, 1995

To GARRY SHANDLING
EL JÉFE
Forty years of shake
rattle & roles —
Transformed into an
overnite success due
to the alchemy of
your genius.
Mi familia y yo
deciámos: ¡Gracias
por todo Patron!

Rip Torn

GARRY We took a season to write pieces of it. And Pete [Tolan] would send me pages and then we'd talk about it. And I said, "Hey, there should be something in there, Pete, where he has to see the people that he fired as he walks down the hallway." And then Pete just wrote it. And everybody was shocked. We had Linda Doucett back, and she doesn't let go of Larry's hand as he's going by. It's really great character stuff.

I'm really proud and happy that amount of effort resulted in anything that's close to being good. I can't imagine the pain of working that hard and it being . . . literally bad. Or meaningless. But then, you know, there would be a reason for that and we would deal with it. I have plenty of that to deal with in other ways, I suppose.

This is how
I'll
be
remembered

GARRY HBO would have carried the show as long as I think I wanted to do it. But the choice of finishing the show was purely mine, and it was a good opportunity to see Larry have to make a choice to some degree over whether he was going to continue to go through hell or to move on with his life.

GARRY I had just done *Hurlyburly* with Sean Penn. And I never have the courage to ask somebody to do the show—ever. I always write a note that says, "I'll respect you more if you pass." And we were on the set and I said to Sean, "Would you ever consider doing the show?" And he said yeah. And then I wrote that part where he says, "That Shandling, man, he was in the trailer talking to my wife. He had a hundred acting coaches." I mean, nobody could beat me up better than I can.

JUDD After six years of asking Jim Carrey to do *The Larry Sanders Show*, I just called him and said, "This is the last show, so you can't delay us." And Jim said something very funny. He said, "I'll do it, but only if I can be the best person who's ever done this." And I'm like, "All right, Jim. We'll try." And he kind of was!

JIM CARREY (actor) I jump on the train at the end. And I go, *Okay. I want to be on the train, but on the train in a way that feels special in some way.* It just was a legendary show. So for me, that was a great, incredible honor for me. That was a real honor. Because of everything. And it was so much incredible fun. I just went out of there that night feeling like, *I'm part of the gang.* I'm such a loner, and that night I felt like I was part of the gang. It was ridiculous. I really thought I had gone too far, and it was too far. But that was kind of the point.

                         LARRY
              Jim Carrey, ladies and gentleman. We'll
              be right back.

                                                            CUT TO:

       FILM:

22   INT. TALK SHOW SET - CONTINUOUS   22

                         STAGE MANAGER (O.S.)
              We're clear.

                         LARRY
              Wow. Thank you so much for doing this,
              Jim. I'm just so thrilled.

                         JIM CARREY
              Let's cut the crap, Larry. Okay?

                         LARRY
              What?

                         JIM CARREY
              You never even liked my work 'till I got
              hugely famous. You're one of those
              intellectual comedians. I'm just too
              broad for your sensibilities.

                         LARRY
              That's not true.

                         JIM CARREY
              What are you going to do now? Movies.
              I'll crush you.

                         LARRY
              Now I can't tell if you're doing a bit.

                         JIM CARREY
              Larry, we're off the air. This is real
              life now. Let me clue you into
              something. I'm only here for three
              reasons: Last show, big ratings, new
              movie. Bim, bam, boom. Otherwise I'd be
              home watching "Nightline" as usual.

                    LARRY
          Who's in it?

                    SEAN PENN
          Kevin Spacey, Anna Paquin...

                    LARRY
          And please don't tell me they're the love
          interest.

                    SEAN PENN
          No. Chazz Palminteri, Meg Ryan and Garry
          Shandling. And myself.

                    LARRY
          And it was a good cast?

                    SEAN PENN
          Yeah. You've got the full spectrum there
          in terms of acting ability.

                    LARRY
          Who was at the low end?

                    SEAN PENN
          Why would I tell you that? I'm not going
          to badmouth anybody in the cast.

                    LARRY
          It's Shandling, right?

                    SEAN PENN
          I'm not going to say. I mean, that guy's
          got enough problems. My wife had a small
          part in the movie? He wouldn't leave her
          alone.

                    LARRY
          Yeah, we had him on the show once and
          he's crazy.

                    SEAN PENN
          It was sad more than anything else. He's
          kind of a pathetic guy.

                    LARRY
          Yeah, let's take a break. Tom Petty's up
          next, so don't go away.

The band plays and the audience applauds.

                                              CUT TO:

Clint Black enters.

                  CLINT BLACK
         Tom, listen. I don't know what everybody
         else was told, but they said I was going
         to sing good-bye to him.

                  TOM PETTY
         Quiet down, cowboy. I'm talking to
         Artie.

                  CLINT BLACK
         Those were their exact words. They have
         to keep their word.

                  TOM PETTY
         I thought I was your Bette Midler. This
         is bullshit.

                  ARTHUR
         Fellas, settle down now. I'm sure we can
         reach some sort of agreement.

Greg Kinnear walks over.

                  GREG KINNEAR
         What are you ~~complaing~~ about? ~~All I~~ get
         to ~~do is walk out and wave like~~ I'm
         ~~fucking Regis Philbin.~~

                  TOM PETTY
         Was I talking to you?

                  GREG KINNEAR
         You are now.

                  CLINT BLACK
           (to Tom)
         Show the man some respect. He was
         nominated for an Academy Award.

                  TOM PETTY
         For what, Talk Soup?

                  ARTHUR
         Everyone, please? I haven't seen so much
         fighting since the Stones played
         Altamont. Thomas?

Arthur cocks his head. He and Tom huddle in the corner.

                                  (CONTINUED)

All you wanted to do was be funny. Be funny in the most authentic way possible: the message will be felt.

1998

June 15
The show is finished. Thank God. What a terrific accomplishment. Your last episode was great. Now you have your movie, Warren's movie and your book.

"Everybody Has a Curtain": *The Larry Sanders Show*

The staffers hurry away. Arthur looks around, opens a nearby
door and exits inside. A beat, then we hear loud sobs from
behind the door.

                                                    CUT TO:

VIDEO:

37   INT. TALK SHOW SET - DURING THE SHOW (NIGHT 2)   37

Larry sits on a stool and takes a beat before speaking.

                    LARRY
          Television is a risky business. You want
          to entertain. You want to do something a
          little different. You want to say things
          that haven't been said before, or show
          things that haven't been seen. Well, you
          try to do all those things, but nine
          times out of ten you end up with "The
          Ropers." It's just the way it is. But I
          think this show wasn't one of the nine
          times. And I have a lot of very talented
          people to thank for that. Artie, without
          a doubt the finest producer who's ever
          guided a pain-in-the-ass star through ten
          years of television. Mr. Hank Kingsley,
          a funny man and a good friend. My
          assistant Beverly. Phil and all the rest
          of the writers. The crew, the staff in
          the office. This show never could have
          happened without them. I'll miss them,
          but I'm comforted to know that none of
          them has my home number.
                    (a beat)
          Thank you for watching. And for allowing
          us to entertain you, and in the case of
          Jim Carrey this evening, to sing things
          that haven't been sung before. I'll tell
          you the truth. I don't know exactly what
          I'm going to do without you.
                    (a beat)
          Goodbye. God bless you. And you may now
          flip.

The band plays the theme one last time. The audience stands
and cheers. Larry does not move from the stool.

                                                    CUT TO:

SARAH SILVERMAN I think I can say this with 99 percent positivity: I was obsessed with "Will You Love Me Tomorrow"—the Carole King version—and I remember playing it for him and it was right around that time, and then he had Shawn Colvin record it for the end and I was so moved, like I couldn't believe it. But it was the perfect song for the end of that show and for everything that it was about.

PETER TOLAN Some of it came later. Jim Carrey and that whole piece of it. But a lot of the other stuff and the structure of it, he and I talked about it, but I wrote the first draft and I said, "I know how it ends, and you're going to love it. I know how it ends, I'm sure of it." But I didn't tell him what it was.

I sat at my computer and I took a Post-it note and I wrote the word "Love" on it. Love. Because I just wanted to remember this last time how much I loved the experience, how much I loved the characters, how much the characters loved each other. In spite of everything. And how much they needed each other, and what the experience had meant to them as the show was breaking up. And wrote it. And gave it to him. And he loved it. He just loved the end of it. The scene with the three men. We used to call them "the troika." When in doubt, just go to the troika. Put the three guys together and something is going to happen. So I knew I had to end it there.

JUDD On the last night, there was a lot of tension and when it was time to do the last scene with you and Rip—

JEFFREY TAMBOR He wanted to pull the plug that night.

JUDD Yes, he did. Garry just noticed that it was about seven or eight pages and he said, "I think it's too long." He was running out of gas and wanted to cut it in half.

JEFFREY I remember we got it in one take . . . and probably he just didn't want to even face it.

Left it all on the field
Left it all on TV.

BRUCE GRAYSON He was so intense shooting that last scene, when he was saying goodbye to the audience, alone on a stool center stage like Carson. I'll never forget it. He released the paid audience because he didn't feel he nailed the closing speech. He kicked everyone off the stage. You could almost feel the energy coming off his body. At one point I thought he was gonna— Well, I mean he did cry in the last scene. He got to that point. He was trying to build himself up. He was angry at the audience. He was determined to get it right, but had to build himself up emotionally. I remember being backstage and he was, like, shaking.

"You may now flip."
—LARRY

"WHAT COULD GO WRONG?": GARRY MAKES SOME MOVIES

Film was still the cooler older sibling to television's nerdy stepbrother when Garry attempted his leap to the big screen. He was initially cast in supporting roles, including by friend Warren Beatty, who brought him aboard his films *Love Affair* and *Town & Country*.

BRIAN LINEHAM (television host) You say that "acting is hard for me because I'm still learning to feel instead of verbalize."

GARRY That's right.

BRIAN Where are you now?

GARRY Well, you know, I think I'm getting better at it. I find myself having to cover less with my comedy than I used to. And that's why it's a challenge for me. And that's why I wanted to act, because I think I can grow as a person through it. Maybe not. Well, let's hope I can. You make me uncomfortable. I don't know why. 1994

2004

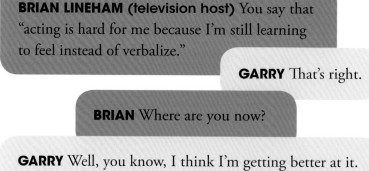

For movie scene:

Feel space and energy between people. Feel room. Act to get what you want. Stay within yourself. Operate from joy.

"What Could Go Wrong?": Garry Makes Some Movies

It doesn't matter if
I can't act in movies,
There's no difference in
TV and movies.
What difference doe
any of it make. The
acting is a commitment
to yourself. It the
betrayal of self that
bothers you!

PETER TOLAN We know Garry as a really great writer, and obviously as a stand-up and all that. But I think if Garry had his wish come true he would be a great actor. That was the thing for him that I think he felt like was out of his grasp. He worked so hard with Roy. And that was just such a goal for him, to be taken seriously as an actor.

"It was Shandling. This guy, unbelievable. The most insecure man I've ever met in my life. Has no focus at all. If our director, Tony Drazan, would even say 'Cut,' he'd look at me and say, 'How was I?' And it didn't stop there. I don't know if he knew if my wife and I were together or what it was, but he was constantly after her, trying to get into her trailer. And then he's got like two hundred acting coaches around. I got to set the first day, I thought they were extras."

—**SEAN PENN,** on the series finale of *The Larry Sanders Show*

Mar. 9

I have finally shifted to my acting. I see on the screen that something cisn't right, And critics agree, when I play parts with no edge or don't feel loose, free, out of control, strong, not fragmented, it doesn't work. I don't love doing it. If I don't have fun and entertain, it doesn't work. make sure you do on x-file – entertain Duchovny, Entertain W.B.

Opposite: Garry and David Duchovny on the set of *The X-Files* episode "Hollywood A.D."

DAVID DUCHOVNY I would sometimes just want him to throw it away. Like when he came and he did a part on *The X-Files* that I wrote and I directed him in, he was supposed to play my character Mulder in the scene, so he was supposed to be this FBI guy running around with a gun. And we were shooting the scene and it was going okay, but it was clunky, it wasn't firing completely right, and I was talking to him about it, and he said, "I can't, I'm not this guy.

I'm not FBI, I'm not Bruce Willis." And I was just thinking, *Well, just fucking fake it,* you know? It's a comedy really. Just fake it. But Garry could not do that, and the fact that he would bring that to bear on the show, on that scene—his own deep insecurity about not being that hero—was so beautiful and heartbreaking to me. I don't know that I could use it or help him, but he's so honest. He couldn't just go, *Hey, I got a gun, I'm gonna fucking do this.*

"What Could Go Wrong?": Garry Makes Some Movies

WHO'S AFRAID OF MIKE NICHOLS?

By all accounts it should have been a success: a comedy co-written by Garry, co-starring Annette Bening, Greg Kinnear, Ben Kingsley, and John Goodman, and directed by one of the greatest comedic helmsmen of all time, Mike Nichols. Unfortunately, creative disharmony on the set of *What Planet Are You From?* helped turn Garry's first major motion picture into his first real brush with failure.

Who is hurt by
Mike Nicols. Who
needs his approval?
Who needs anyone's
approval...Who?
I'm just trying
to be free and committed
in my acting and not
be concerned about
that. But if I want
him to approve of me,
he will not. You
don't approve of him
and yet you want him
to approve of you.

1999

"What Could Go Wrong?": Garry Makes Some Movies

PETER TOLAN They started shooting in Phoenix, and at the end of day one, I get a call from Mike saying, "Get down here." I took a quick flight to get down there and I said, "What's going on?" And he said, "What is he doing? I don't have time for him to find a performance. He wrote this. He should know how to do it." And he wanted Garry to do it in two takes.

ED SOLOMON It was an expensive movie, and Mike Nichols was getting paid a shit ton of money, which I think is the only reason he did the movie. Basically it's about a guy from another planet who is told he needs to go down to Earth and impregnate somebody. And, in order to impregnate her, he has to somehow infiltrate himself into her life by acting like he's romantically interested. And then getting involved in a domestic type of a relationship, and seeing if he can, in fact, find love.

FADE IN ON

INT. A DARKENED ROOM ON A DISTANT PLANET

An attractive HOLOGRAM WOMAN (naked) rotates in the center
of the room. A male ROBOTIC VOICE speaks:

                  ROBOTIC VOICE
        The Earth woman's reproductive organs
        are located here.

Three blue lights pulse on the HOLOGRAM WOMAN, indicating
her ovaries and uterus.

                  ROBOTIC VOICE
        The access is here.
            (a green light pulses on)
        Insertion is here and here only.
        Insertion anywhere else will not result
        in pregnancy. A woman on birth control
        pills or another form of contraception--

A MAN'S VOICE is heard:

                  MAN'S VOICE
        Repeat.

The man sits in a chair; sensor wires are attached to his
forehead. He's concentrating hard, studying the HOLOGRAM.
Call him HAROLD.

                  ROBOTIC VOICE
        A woman on birth control--

                  HAROLD
        No. Repeat and clarify the part about
        insertion.

                  ROBOTIC VOICE
        Insertion is here and here only.
            (a green light pulses)
        Insertion anywhere else will not result
        in pregnancy.

Red lights pulse on in the non-insertion areas: the mouth,
the anus, between the breasts, and in the space next to the
Hologram woman's head.

                  HAROLD
        What is that area?

                                            (CONTINUED)

CONTINUED:

                    ROBOTIC VOICE
          The pillow.

                    HAROLD
          Understood. And how exactly do I get
          the woman in the mood for insertion?

                    ROBOTIC VOICE
                (a long silence)
          Searching.
                (another pause)
          Still searching
                (pause)
          That code has not been broken. All that
          is known is, the woman becomes more
          receptive when complimented on these
          areas.

The HOLOGRAM WOMAN'S hair, brain, eyes, lips, breasts,
waist, behind, legs, and feet light up in that order.

                    ROBOTIC VOICE
          She also likes to be told that her shoes
          are fashionable, that her hair looks
          lovely that way, and that her dress is a
          knockout.

                                        DISSOLVE TO:

INT. A DARKENED ROOM ON A DISTANT PLANET - DAYS LATER

HAROLD dances with the HOLOGRAM WOMAN, the music stops.

                    HAROLD
                (to Hologram)
          You're so light on your feet. Would you
          like to go somewhere quiet where we can
          talk?

                    HOLOGRAM WOMAN
          Let's go back to my place.

                    HAROLD
          Okay. Thanks.

The HOLOGRAM WOMAN shrinks to a hovering spot of light.
HAROLD takes his seat.

                    ROBOTIC VOICE
          Congratulations. This completes your
          training. You have attained a perfect
          score.

                                        (CONTINUED)

CONTINUED:

The room illuminates, becoming very white and seemingly
without dimension. Pull back from HAROLD to reveal another
man observing him. He's older, serious, dressed in a black
uniform of some sort, made of material not yet discovered on
Earth. He's the leader of the planet--GRAYDON. He looks to
someone standing next to him and nods.

                                                    CUT TO:

INT. WHITE CORRIDOR

GRAYDON walks with HAROLD down a tubular concourse.

                    GRAYDON
          We're five times more intelligent than
          humans. Anything we don't know, you'll
          be able to figure out easily once you're
          there.

                    HAROLD
          Good.

                    GRAYDON
          Extrapolating from your score in the
          simulator, it should take you exactly
          ten days to impregnate a woman.

                    HAROLD
          Good.

                    GRAYDON
          We are on our way to creating a
          homogeneous universe, in which there
          will be no wars or conflicts of any
          kind, because we will all be the same.

                    HAROLD
          Like you and me.

GRAYDON nods. They simultaneously turn away and bend down
to tie their shoes.

                    GRAYDON
          Don't be discovered for who you are.
          That means no use of our technology, and
          no contact with us once you're there.

                    HAROLD
          Of course.

They both finish tying their shoes and stand.

                                              (CONTINUED)

BRUCE GRAYSON Garry always felt like he got good after take five, or take three. It became more conversational. And because he never had a lot of confidence in his acting, he didn't think he was as good. He thought he could get good. And he thought he was getting better, and working with Rip—that cast was fantastic—but he thought that he was learning things, and what he really wanted to concentrate on was his acting. So when he got into the ring with Mike Nichols, and Mike basically would do two takes—one take sometimes—and say, "We're moving on!," he was just getting into it. He wouldn't let Garry rewrite. And Garry goes, "This can only get better." He would make his case. And Mike goes, "You know, we didn't do *The Graduate* that way."

Garry's trademark wince is as prominent as ever opposite director Mike Nichols.

"What Could Go Wrong?": Garry Makes Some Movies

M , Nicole
M Nicol —
M Nico —
M, Nic —
M, Ni
M, M —
M. —

n —

—

He's dark. Don't give him your mind by trying to figure it out. Go on to your next moment. Be everything you can be. Compassionate, Giving, Funny, Meditate, Clean

ED SOLOMON Garry described an experience that's still to this day one of the most painful things I've heard, and I heard other people describe it too. There was a moment when I think Mike looked at—either it was the first playback or the first set of dailies—and just looked at Garry and went like, "Oh my God," like, just had a physical, visceral reaction that was negative. And Garry knew it. From the beginning, day one, it was just a toxic, unsafe environment for him, and it was painful for him. Because Garry always used people as touch points. To echolocate or to orientate himself. He was just looking to get some sense of sonar about, like, *Where am I?* When suddenly the director isn't reflecting back to him, but rather closes off to him, it sent him into a panic. It sent him into a free fall. And of course, as you know, you can't do comedy from that.

PETER TOLAN He's resorting to calling him "Garry Shambling." In front of me. To anybody. He would be mean.

Mimi S

On my way back to Hawaii. Feb 13 is when I left. That's 3 weeks ago. I did 2½ weeks of solid press. I only have 9 days. Then I have to do X Files and Town + Country. God. (Don't forget "Doings" for Town + County)

I can't describe the pain/depression/emptiness/sadness of knowing how badly

my movie did and how weak it is and what the reviews were and what Nicols did to it and how I knew it all..

It bombed at the box office. It got a few good reviews. It's embarrassing to me, I have to put it

behind me like a bad Tonite show or a bad game. The good news is that eventually people forget. They forget the good work as well as the bad. They'll forget your T.V. shows and eventually they'll forget this movie. It's all about present moment. Enjoy Hawaii. Be good to yourself.

JAMES L. BROOKS (writer/director) We used to go to lunch—Michael, Garry, and I—and he was valiant. He was valiant. And I'd be in such a funny spot, because I'd hear the word-for-word what happened on the set, and it wasn't the Mike I knew at all, but holy shit—whoever was doing it to him, I don't know how you could have a rougher time as an actor starring in a movie he had written. I can't imagine a tougher experience. It's just so awkward for me. Mike Nichols is one of the greatest men who ever lived. I believe Garry was too. But Garry was in an unfamiliar and totally vulnerable situation. And I think Mike must've felt similarly trapped.

doing your best was your job. You failed professionally. Professionally you should have <u>made</u> it all work: the relationship, the movie, the <u>acting</u>. You could have, had you had the power and experience done something. This is a defeat. You couldn't even get the movie ad changed at the end. This is a loss, A death. You didn't win. You lost. Now you have to put this game behind you like an athlete-accept the loss and pick yourself up and use what you've learned. After a loss a team looks dejected. They feel the loss. Make sure that you feel this loss. Then they look at the films and go back out onto the court. No one wins

1999

Movies

'Planet' crashes, burns with its tired storyline

By CHRIS HEWITT
Knight Ridder News Service

Enough already with movies about privileged, middle-aged guys who

Kingsley). Shandling and Bening, real-life friends, are great together.

But for every clever line, there's an obvious, sophomoric bit, like when

REVIEW

Playing at Bonita Springs 12, Bonita Springs; Coralwood 10, Cape Coral; Hollywood 20, Naples; Merchants Crossing 16, North Fort Myers; Naples Twin Drive In, Naples; Northside Drive In, Noprth Fort Myers; Pavilion

---

Shandling leaves 'Planet' lifeless

Stars:

★

R (for sexuality and lan-

By Roger Ebert
UNIVERSAL PRESS SYNDICATE

Here is the most uncomfortable movie of the new year, an exercise in feel-good smut. "What Planet Are You From?" starts out as a

Garry Shandling is a space alien who is on Earth to impregnate a woman (Annette Bening) in the new comedy "What Planet Are You From?"

Columbia Pictures

MOVIES

Spaced-out mess

With 'Planet,' Shandling ruins even simplest comic premise

By JEFFREY WESTHOFF
The Northwest Herald

What once worked for Jerry Lewis, Robin Williams and Jeff Bridges doesn't come close to working for Garry Shandling.

Shandling, who conceived the story and co-wrote the script for "What Planet Are You From?"

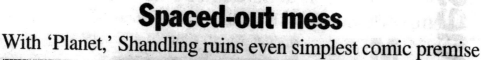

QUICK TAKE

"What Planet Are You From?"
★

Rated R for sexuality and language
Running time: 1 hour, 40 minutes
Written by Garry Shandling, Michael Leeson, Ed Solomon and Peter Tolan

---

MOVIES

Too many jokes go limp

Real humor is alien, and Garry Shandling doesn't help any

By Jay Boyar
SENTINEL MOVIE CRITIC

Talk about high-concept!
An alien from a technologically advanced, all-male planet comes to Earth on a mission to impregnate one of our women with his synthetic penis.
Just imagine how the eyes of the executives at Columbia Pictures must have twinkled when director Mike Nichols (The

REVIEW

'What Planet Are You From?'
★★

Cast: Garry Shandling, Annette Bening, John Goodman, Greg Kinnear, Ben Kingsley, Linda Fiorentino.
Director: Mike Nichols.
Screenwriters: Garry Shandling, Michael Leeson, Ed Solomon, Peter Tolan.
Cinematographer: Michael Ballhaus.
Music: Carter Burwell.
Running time: 1 hour, 40 minutes.
Industry rating: R (restricted)

Parents' guide: Sexuality

"I'm his best buddy on earth."
            Greg Kinnear

"I tried my darndest to pull this off."
            G.S.

"I thought we could do it."
            A.B. we all make mistakes

"That the last time I trust my instinct."
            G.K.

"I moved back to England when we wrapped. B.K.

"I'm the Alien"
            G.S.

"I'm the woman he tries to impregnate."
            A.B.

"I'm the guy chasing him."
            John Goodman

"I'm the leader of the other other planet." Ben Kingsley

"I hate all of these people. M.N.

"I never quite understood my role. G.K.

PETER TOLAN One thing about Garry—I don't think he was ever delusional. So I don't think he was saying, *I'm going to do this movie and I'm going to become a movie star.* Or, *I'm going to become a serious actor and I'm going to get these parts and I'm going to do this.* No, he did some of that later on, but it was sort of hodgepodge. He may have thought, *I'm going to have this new thing. Which might be a little more manageable for me. As opposed to being the guy in charge, why don't I be an actor and just go and maybe tweak a few of my lines, but that's my day. Just do the scene,* because he loved that challenge. So why not have that be your career instead of being the guy that it's all on your shoulders? And then he has the experience and it turns out miserably and he just goes, *Well, I don't know what to do now.*

"I hate watching
myself."
            G.S
"

I thought, Mike
Nicols, Gary Shandling,
Greg turriero, Ben Kingsley,
Annite Bening ... what
could go wrong?
Wait till you see.
            John
            Goodman

"I think this movie
is painless and goes
by quickly."
            G.S

"I love this movie.
What the name of
it?"
            Annite Bening

"I have a very,
very good feeling about
this movie."
            Ben Kingsley
"I   "This is the end of my career.
"I love movies and Greg
this is one!"   Kner
            John Goodman
I never laugh out loud at
movies but I almost did at this one.

"I loved working with Annette Benning, John Goodman and Ben Kingsley. They were hilarious."
G.S

"I loved working with Ben Kingsley and John Goodman, they are such talented actors.
Annette Benning

"I love working"
Ben Kingsley

"What part did Shandling play?"
John Goodman

AD CAMPAIGN:

"I don't think I'm that good in the movie, but the story is hilarious."
GARRY SHANDLING

"I think Gerry Shandling is good in the movie and I'm not okay, But one thing is for sure: the story is hilarious."
Annette Benning

"I'm hilarious and the story is hilarious."
Ben Kingsley

"I'm in it and I can't wait to see it!"
JOHN GOODMAN

The story of a man from another world who finds himself on Earth. A real comedy.

1999

341

GARRY'S THIRD ACT

With a couple of bad movie experiences in his rearview, Garry returned to the comfort of the two things he knew best: hosting and television. He played master of ceremonies at the Emmy Awards twice, in 2000 and 2004, pouring all his remaining creative energies into the job.

DAVID DUCHOVNY When he hosted the Emmys, it was a nightmare to be his friend during that time, because he spent the entire year preparing for what I'm gonna say is a silly gig.

2000

July 10

Do the best, most original, most honest, funniest, classiest emmy's. Be Centered, strong, honest, reverent, irreverent, funny, serious, kind, loving and giving.

Writing is very easy. You open up / pick up a piece of blank paper or open a new file —

I still write longhand although I keep a ~~laptop~~ laptop sitting on me because I like the pressure on my lap.

Face a blank page and start writing jokes. Chihuahuas - I think I have Age

this is the last Emmy of the millennium. I'm sick of it. Y2K will take it away. Everything is the last of the millennium. This won't got exposes us because

How can you lose when you're presenting? They don't let you give it away. To model - see - you did that perfect - you were so worried.

Laser Surgery — Mr Cosby
Lap Top   Scrubs said
Messy   Hey don't
Chihuahuas   pull me into this.
— couch.
Making movies Glasses
They don't come out
for a year. T.V.
you shoot it. Its
on the air - your
cancelled all
in Two months.
I nstant Gratification.

The Always a pleasure
this year is great because
I don't have to worry
about losing. I have
65 acceptance speeches never used
for sale.
Presenting is even more an
honor than winning or getting
nominated. Anyone can be
nominated.

2000

GAVIN DE BECKER The first Emmys that he did, which was the sort of *Sanders* Emmys, was highly irreverent of awards shows. And then on the second one, he was taking on reality shows in a big way and really poking fun at television all the time. And you're not going to get help inside the industry for that. What he typically got is "I wouldn't do that, Garry." Or even an agent would say, "That might be going a little far." He wanted to go far. He just didn't buy the reverence piece at all. And he somehow had the ability to get them to trust him that it would work. And both of those last two Emmys that he did were risky as hell. They were doing things that people just did not do on awards shows, and that's the only thing that made it fun for him.

Sept 19
Emmies;

Warrior - bea
willing to die.
Use everything.
stay empty, Light,
HAVE FUN,
Masculine,
Frenny, loose
tight, connected
to audience.
MU. Within
yourself, PRESENT
stripped down,
Audience, you,
stage + jokes - all

I have a full life
yoga
Emmies 3500 most
emmies / TV
VS
Everyone's excited MOVIE
at first / First 5 hours /
2 show - 25 million /
It changed Oeeer uge /
opposite sex / Talk
to dead relatives /
Hitler - Larry David -
Osama Bin Laden
Ray Romano last
get to know myself
season - GOD Doesn't
know you exist / Space
program
Buddha not married
→ Penis I'll be
Eye loses broke family
Violence / Kids man
Yoga class in Somalia

Above:
Notes for
Garry's Emmy
broadcasts.

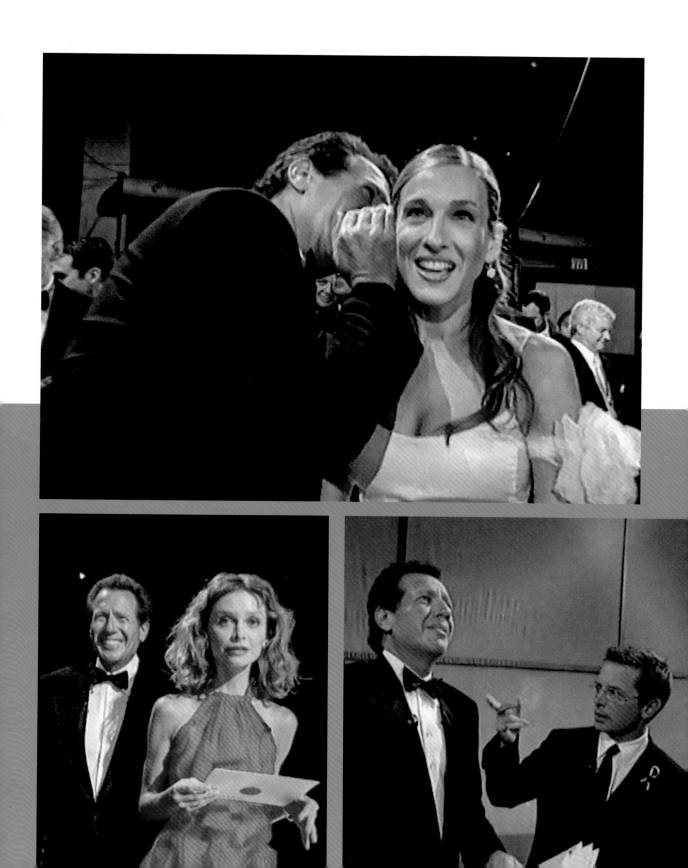

GARRY I hosted the Emmys in 2000, which is right when I ended the *Sanders* show and everything. There I was, doing four hours on live TV, and my buddy was with me in the dressing room when I came offstage, and I sat down in a chair and I said, "I think that's it for a while." And I realized I just hadn't stopped.

I will not do any Michael Jackson jokes. I leave that to your fellow musician Jerry Lee Lewis, who said, "Hey, what's the big deal? The kid wasn't even related to him."

evaluation. You couldn't stay on a dead run — dating + working. you've hosted and done the Tonight show. you've done 3 specials 2 series — award winning — won an Emmy. Wrote a movie — made a bad one · T and country — and hosted the emmies. you've done 155 episode of ½ T.V. and stand-up. you dated a lot. you've lived a full life and

2000

accomplished so much —
from not being in
show business at all —
to taking it on
and succeeding. You
knew no one here
25 years ago. (And wrote
scripts for Sanford +
son + Welcome Back
Kotter.) You had to
take a break from
everything. Now in
this break, you
can get in touch with
all of this and what is
next... to slowly get
strong emotionally and

I love *The Sopranos*.
It's a fantastic show.
Here's what flipped
me out: In the
first episode, Tony
Soprano's mother
is literally planning
to have him
killed. That's why
I admire Italian
women. Jewish
moms drag
it out a whole
lifetime.

D6   THE NEWS JOURNAL ··· TUESDAY, SEPT. 12, 2000

It was Garry Shandling's Emmys, thank goodness

By FRAZIER MOORE
Associated Press

NEW YORK — "I said to my mother, 'I'm hosting the Emmys,'" cracked Garry Shandling. "She said, 'You do what you have to do.'"

Thank goodness he did.

Neurotic, self-embarrassed and fearlessly ironic, Shandling turned Sunday's Emmycast into a one-man show.

Aired live on ABC from Los Angeles' Shrine Auditorium, "The 52nd Annual Primetime Emmy Awards" was what it always is; an overlong display of gussied-up stars and mostly hollow tributes.

This year, no problem. Even when absent from the handsome grids-and-cubes stage setting, Shandling drolly ruled. With his wry stewardship, he kept everything honest.

"You know what slows this show down?" he mused. "Seriously: the awards. They should

AP/MARK J. TERRILL
Quipped Garry Shandling during the Emmycast: "I read for the part of vice president [on 'The West Wing']. They said, 'Too Jewish.'"

At another point, he yanked things into perspective again by introducing a few TV clips "overlooked by the Academy": "overlooked by the Academy": monster truck races, "Jerry monster truck races, "Jerry Springer," Weather Channel forecasts and a woman hawking watches on Home Shopping Network.

He did a quick, apparently off-the-cuff interview with the onstage "trophy girl."

"I started as a trophy girl," he told her. "And now I'm host."

And in a backhanded compliment to the cable network that aired his bygone comedy series "The Larry Sanders Show," Shandling observed that an acceptance speech could go on for days if HBO, rather than ABC, were airing the Emmys.

Shandling's style of keeping it real (or at least an irreverent facsimile of real) proved infectious.

Former "Seinfeld" player Michael Richards delivered a lengthy, impassioned thank-you speech for having been chosen by the Academy as a presenter, seeming to forget all about presenting the award.

Even Michael J. Fox made sport of his Parkinson's tremors in a mock-impromptu backstage encounter with Shandling.

"Your tie is all screwed up," Fox told him.

"Could you fix it?" Shandling asked.

"Believe me," warned Fox, producing his shaky hands, "you don't want ..."

Later, no one could have failed to be touched by Fox's brief but heartfelt acceptance for his best comedy actor award.

Veteran actor Jack Lemmon, who won for his performance in the TV film "Oprah Winfrey Presents: Tuesdays With Morrie," also won himself a standing ovation.

Each of them elegantly gowned and great with child, tandem presenters Jane Leeves ("Frasier") and Kelli Williams ("The Practice") made a lovely sight.

And presenter Cher, as always a welcome addition, scored with her dyed-blond tresses and accompanying dumb-blonde joke.

But the night belonged to Shandling, who even put his imprint on the night's biggest winner, the White House drama "The West Wing."

"I read for the part of vice president," he disclosed. "They said, 'Too Jewish.'"

The season past was an odd one whose biggest craze, reality TV, flew under the Academy's radar. But not Shandling's.

To prove it, the Emmycast (which Shandling said ABC considered renaming "Who Wants to Win an Emmy?") began up roariously with a taped sketch spoofing CBS' summer smash "Survivor."

In a setting that looked exactly like remote Pulau Tiga, "Survivor" host Jeff Probst convened a tribal council to decide who would host the Emmy show (and receive the Pontiac Aztec.)

Among Shandling's fellow castaways were Arsenio Hall, who complained that Shandling was "walking around buck naked on the island," and Craig Kilborn of "The Late, Late Show."

When the votes were counted, it was Shandling who was chosen.

"Can I just take the car?" he begged Probst.

"No, Garry, you have to host."

If viewers are lucky, he'll have to host again next year.

TALK SHOWS

24 hour listings appear in Sunday TV Book.
News / Talk/ Business
12:00
Movies   Sports

Daytime

Garry's Third Act

GARRY My life had been devoted completely to stand-up and chasing women and doing the things a man shouldn't do after probably the age of forty-nine, so that was the perfect time for me to readjust. Except what I really did is, I hadn't really lived, I'd devoted myself to working, so then I started traveling and leading a life that involved relationships, good relationships with people.

Let go of what Fully, Planet are you from.

Do you have the courage to put all "this" aside—drop it, & let it go. Are you willing to let it go.— like a kite — let go of the string — let go of the string — open up your hands, your "grip" and let it all go.

2001

GAVIN DE BECKER If you're in Los Angeles, people expect to see you a lot, and they're gonna see you at this event or that event, and he didn't chase the common prizes, in terms of running around and doing another TV series when he could have, hosting a talk show when he could have, hosting *The Tonight Show* when he could have. He just didn't do it the regular way, so people found him to be mysterious and unusual. He had a good line once. Somebody came up—we were in a restaurant somewhere—and said, "Are you gonna do anything after *Sanders*?" And he said, "What, that wasn't good enough?"

June 3 - Hawaii
Wow. 58.
Sitting in Hawaii.
Watched MTV
Movie Awards
2008 - I am out
of that world -
Not in. Don't

View life as
more exciting (maybe)
accepting -
way

2008

JIM CARREY I think he was struggling back and forth. Because like all comics, at some point you start going, *Can I survive without it? Who am I without it? What if I left the Mardi Gras mask at home? And I just went to the party without it? Oh, they'd be so disappointed.*

It's fucking terrifying. Because what if the train leaves and you can never get back on? That's the key. *What if it leaves, and I can never get back on?*

JOHN MARKUS Artie Shaw, the greatest clarinet player who ever lived, it took him seven hours a day of practice to maintain that tone and that ability. In 1954 he woke up at the height of his fame and he turned his clarinet into a lamp, never played it again, because he knew he couldn't be what those things were in the past. Garry had hit home runs twice, he had two Super Bowl rings with those shows, and I didn't think he felt he could do it again.

JON FAVREAU (director/actor) I reached out to Garry for *Elf,* he was one of the guys who I wanted before James Caan was cast. And he didn't like at all that he could be Will Ferrell's dad at the time, 'cause remember it was like 2001. So I said, "Mathematically you could, but it doesn't seem like you would, which is what's funny because you don't know you have a son, then it's him." But the conversation never really progressed.

SHOW IDEA

Behind the
scenes with
God.

Angels

Jesus

1998

I'm not one
of those people
who needs
constantly be
on TV to
feel that
he exists

2000

PETER TOLAN After *Sanders* ended, we sold another show. Within the next year. It was called *Life Everlast, Inc.* And it was about the idea that heaven was run like a multinational corporation. So it was like a wall, and you could see everything going on in the world. And he would play God. And he was depressed and *What have I done?* and all that sort of stuff. He liked it and we worked on it, went to HBO, and sold it. And they said, "Great, start writing." And he just never wanted to write. He drifted. It drifted. I didn't push him. But I, at a certain point, was like, "We really should." I got another call. They're anxious to see something. And he's like, "I'm going to go to Hawaii, but I think I'll be ready in like a month." And then the month would go by.

Somebody asked me where I was on 9/11, and I said, "Which 9/11? I've had so many terrible 9/11's."

2014

[handwritten note] If I had a Child Now I would name it. 3JAY:SHA3 NDCING? SO it couldn't be hacked, Its the punctuation in the name that always gets me.

JUDD I was doing a lot of sets with him at Largo, and he would come onstage and he really was trying to be present and almost wasn't as concerned with the ideas as much as something happening. And it's like he didn't care if he had all the jokes. He wanted moments to happen onstage, and he loved the idea that they didn't laugh at all then got home and slowly put it together.

DAVID DUCHOVNY He had this other idea where a guy his age, which would've been in his mid-fifties at the time, in a midlife crisis, checks into an old-age home. And becomes the stud of the old-age home, dominates sports-wise and gets all the ladies. So that was another idea of his that we tossed around for a while and it never went anywhere.

KEVIN NEALON I thought, *Well, I guess he's kind of retired now.* And I was trying to figure out what it was that made him kind of become reclusive to performing again, and there were a couple of things. Maybe it was the whole Brad Grey experience, with the lawsuits and stuff. Or maybe it was one of his movies not doing well. Or maybe he just had enough of it. But he was slowly getting back into it. He liked to perform with us. He liked to get onstage with another comic to begin with at least, to ease him in, and then, you know, take it from there. But he would seem to be a little nervous before he would go on.

Joke

I've been spending my time getting to see what life is like off television. It's awful. I can now tell everyone watching at home — Get on TV, whatever reality show, game show ~~anything~~ whatever it fantastic. This two minute is everything.

2003

BILL ISAACSON There was a very lucky group of people in this town who accidentally saw his stand-up work, because he would go down to the club and he would just decide to do it, and that happened a lot during the last years. That's why there was all this material around. And a thousand people would say to him, "Are you gonna do a stand-up special?" And he would say, "Maybe I should do a stand-up special." But he never seemed to care enough to get around to do that. He seemed happy going through the process at the club.

GARRY What I do now is, I'll stop onstage and I'll let the audience come to a complete stop, which is incredibly awkward. And it'll be dead silent in the club, and I stand there and I let it be silent. Then I say, "Love and wisdom is in that silence." And no one wants to stay in that silence. And they still don't know what to do but they're listening, and then I say, "Let's do it again."

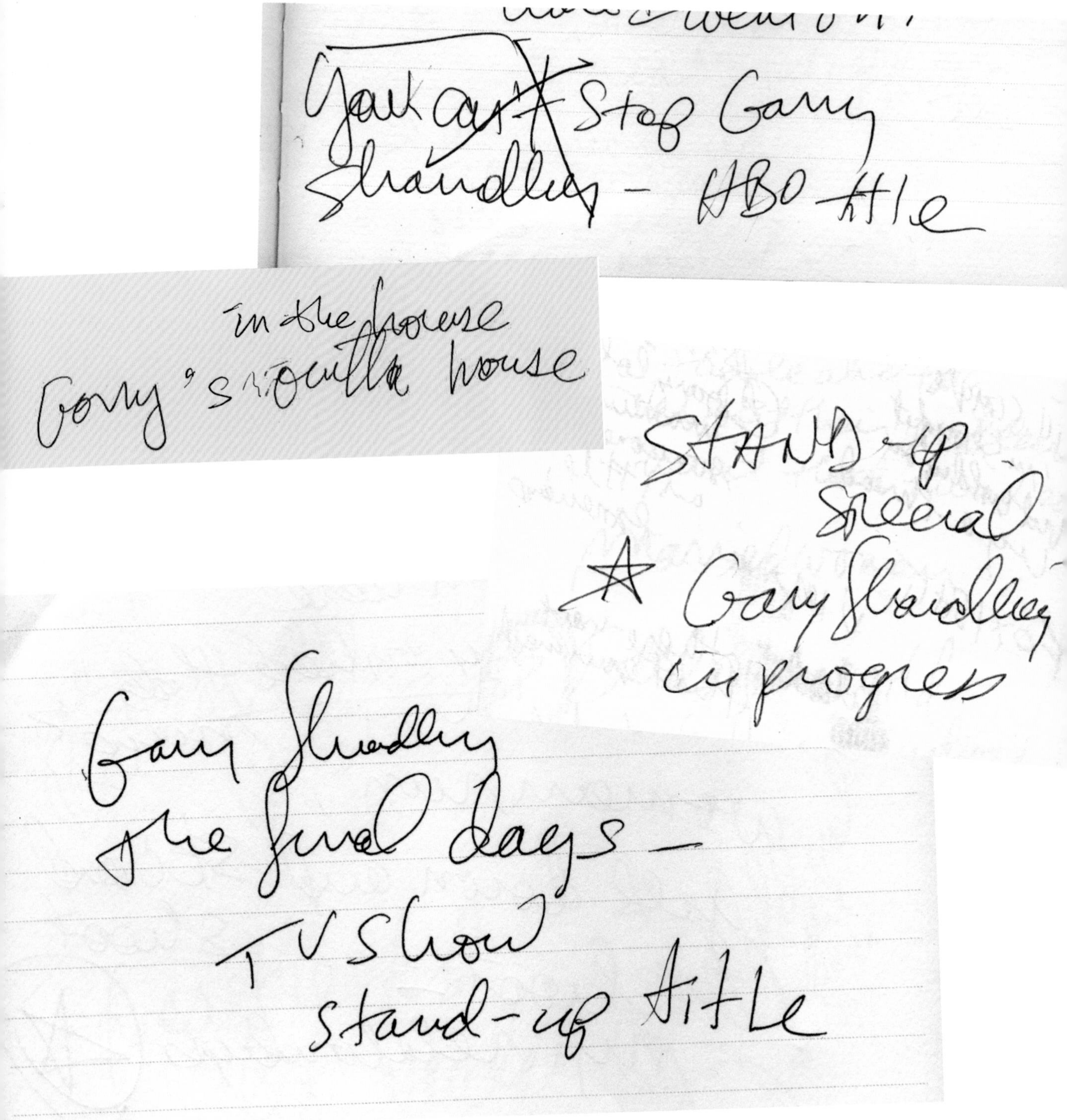

(handwritten notes)

You can't stop Garry Shandling — HBO title

In the house
Garry's gorilla house

STAND-UP Special
★ Gary Shandling in progress

Gary Shandling
The final days —
TV show
stand-up title

Possible titles Garry brainstormed for a new stand-up special that never materialized.

I've been single my
whole life. Eharmony
just matched me
with a gun.

April 24
Killed at Magic
Club in a new,
progressive way.

While never returning to a leading role after *What Planet Are You From?*, Garry occasionally accepted the odd acting job in his later years, including providing the voice of Verne the turtle in 2006's *Over the Hedge* and appearing opposite Robert Downey, Jr., in *Iron Man 2.*

Garry's Third Act

KAREY KIRKPATRICK (director of *Over the Hedge*) I had never worked with a craftsman like that. When I write, I tend to throw a lot of darts. I don't go into the minutiae of a line. I'll spit something out—I come from an improv background, so it's more like just throwing a lot of darts. And then the one that sticks feels right. Garry examined every word. I once heard a story about how Richard Rodgers composed, and he explored every melody combination until he landed on one. And that's what it was like for Garry.

FEMALE SQUIRREL
It's Verne.

MALE SQUIRREL
Typical.

Looking over, Verne sees the squirrel couple sitting sideways in their tipped-over home, glaring angrily.

VERNE
(backing out)
How's it going?

Emerging from the fallen tree, Verne sees the whole forest looking on.

SKINNY FEMALE SKUNK
C'mon Verne, we were sleeping!

VERNE
Uh, I was gathering food for next winter.

AUSTRALIAN POSSUM
Next *winter*?! We're five-and-a-half bloody minutes into spring!

VERNE
Well, you can never be too prepared.

Stepping up, the hungry WEASEL yanks the fern-wrap from Verne's hand and gobbles it down.

Ignoring Verne, other HUNGRY ANIMALS jump down and start chowing down the mint and acorns at his feet.

VERNE
Hello? Anybody heard of "deferred gratification"?

EXT. HEDGE - DAY

WE HEAR A DINOSAUR ROAR coming through the hedge. What looks
like a dinosaur, pops its head out but it is only a hand prop
that R.J. has found. The entire animal community
follows R.J. as he marches towards Barry and Janis's yard.

                    VERNE

          Please - going into that house is
          insane! Their dog will eat you
          alive.
                    R.J.
          Don't be so negative.
               (shouting to the others)
          Am I not the master of suburban
          living?

R.J. walks off across the yard. Frightened to go further,
Verne, Norbert and the others all stop.

                    WILD-EYED WEASEL
               (to R.J.)
          Do it! Take everything you see!

VERNE'S P.O.V.

Forelegs against the glass, the Basset Hound (Max) stands at
a window, barking madly. On the patio, Barry is cleaning the
barbeque. Behind him, the patio door is open. Without a trace
of fear, R.J. strides across the patio, directly behind
Barry, and enters the house.

                                        CUT BACK TO
                    VERNE
          He's in!

Verne turns to see that everyone has moved to get a better
look.

                    VERNE
          Hey, hey! Wait up!

Jan 28
IM2   Tomorrow

1) Gervais
2) See my power (Dont Act powerful)
3) Masculine
4) To get acknowledgment
5) RDJ = Beatty - "we meet again"
6) Cradle - Grab
7) Vote for me
8) Obst = Dont like Stark. (Beatty Felix Award)
9)

2009

BRUCE GRAYSON He would walk into those sessions, angry sometimes, and it would just be hysterical how he would just labor over delivery, the line itself, could we rewrite it—and then you see Bruce Willis in the background just like, "All right, let's do this!"

Above: Garry's notes for playing the antagonistic Senator Stern in *Iron Man 2*.

JON FAVREAU He was watching political stuff and he had been a guest on Tavis Smiley, I think, and we were talking about maybe could Garry be good for this? And I was like, "Garry's the best, I love Garry," and I talked to him and he was like, "It's interesting that you would think of me for that," because it was so different from stuff he had done. He came in there and it was our first day of photography on that and he was just great.

THINKING OUTSIDE THE BOX SET

When it came time to produce the DVD release of *The Larry Sanders Show*, Garry went all in, filming a series of unscripted encounters with former cast, crew, and guest stars that added one final layer to the show's attempt to pan for truth in Hollywood's river of BS.

GARRY This is actually going to make me cry. This is the most fun I've had in a couple years.

TOM PETTY Yeah. I feel good.

GARRY Don't you? Seriously . . .

TOM Yeah, you were under a lot of pressure from time to time.

GARRY It was unbearable.

TOM Yeah, and then you had the lawsuit and the whole . . . I shouldn't mention . . .

GARRY You can! Because we've talked about it. It just made it very hard.

TOM I mean, God, I really felt bad for you. We were both . . . I was getting a divorce and you were getting sued, so we weren't perfect company. You know? We could just bitch endlessly. But it was true. We were just destroyed. And look at you now. I mean, you've come out of it. You're making a DVD.

PETER TOLAN The next time, weirdly, that I saw him as focused in his way was doing the DVD set. Which he put a tremendous amount of energy into. Like a crazy amount of energy. Because it just went on and on and on. And I said, "It's never coming out!"

GARRY Purely I thought, if I'm going to do DVD extras for *Larry Sanders,* the DVD extras have to go somewhere further than the show went, period. The only thing that interested me about those extras was going and talking to those people so intimately.

GAVIN DE BECKER In the last few years, I think he got really comfortable with the idea that he had done enough really great stuff. And the last big creative venture for him was the DVD package for *Sanders,* called *Not Just the Best of the Larry Sanders Show.* Because he really put a lot of energy into that. And that is excellent, the interviews in it. I can't even call them interviews. The conversations that he went around and had with people are so authentic and real and present in the moment, and he really did enjoy that thing a lot. I think it's all the same animal. It's all, *Can I get to the center truth that's inside this thing?* And so his willingness and his openness to go around and have conversations with people that he'd had profound conflict with—the head of his studio, who's dating Linda; Sharon Stone, who he'd had a relationship with and they'd broken up; Jon Stewart, who was on the last couple seasons of the show—and to just talk through everything. It was really like going around and tying a bow on that experience.

As I make the long
Sanders DVD's I
see and feel love

between many, and
the truth of impermance
and the passing of time.
To man drop self-judgment,
and embrace reality, love
and openness. Release self-
judgment and just be →

2005

PETER BERG (filmmaker) I remember coming into the gym and seeing Garry and Alec Baldwin beating the shit out of each other. I didn't know any of this was happening, but Garry had arranged to have Alec come in, and his idea for the interview was *I'm gonna fight him, like really fight him.* And Alec's stronger than Garry, but Alec wasn't in particularly great shape at that time, and I thought they were both having heart attacks. I remember they collapsed on the ring and they were just both sucking air, and I was concerned that one or both of them was gonna die. Then Garry started talking, and he wanted to do the interview after they had beaten the shit out of each other. They were both in their late fifties at the time.

Funny time — strange 2 years —
chose turtle movie and
spent 2 years editing &
shooting DVDs. And time moves
quickly. What to do?
I am still tired.

2006

DAVID DUCHOVNY Garry was a guy that people asked about. If you were known as one of Garry's friends, people would ask you about Garry. Some people were concerned. Some people never understood why he wasn't working more. They would see a guy with all this talent, they go, "Why isn't Garry doing another show?" I feel like that ambition had left him. I hope it did, because I hate to think of him being unhappy that he's not working his ass off. I think he was trying to find the next question that was gonna interest him and whatever form that was gonna take; I think showbiz, the whole rat race of it, I don't know if it really held any interest to him by the end.

GARRY Someone said to me, "Why don't you come back on TV and do another series?" And I said, "Yeah, I'm thinking of doing a reality show called *Oh No, Not Him Again.*"

Garry's Third Act

a good actor or
writer. You don't
need to be happy.
You don't need
to be anything. You
can just be. the
"anything" part is
your ego.

Wish I was
younger? So I could
go thru more years
of what?

1999

GARRY SHANDLING IN PROGRESS

In the end, Garry's most personal and longest-running project wasn't a stand-up routine or a TV show, it was himself. Spirituality and self-improvement were key pillars of his life philosophy and, as he was a Zen Buddhist in Hollywood, it was perhaps inevitable that so much of Garry's writing (both for the screen and in his journals) would grapple with the topic of ego.

Jan 13, 1984

To lead a zen life even when tired and burned out — to be it, accept it. To lead a zen life when even on the road — to become the road — accept it. To love where you're at now. To love who you're with now.

Don't ever be concerned with how other comics are doing compared to you. STOP.

Only you influence what you do.

① July 10

You realize now that comedy is your soul. You are fully being when you're creative and funny. Be all of that. Now you remember, it can't just work. Also,

'suchest in the world. Garry, your strength now is to move on. To live moment-to-moment. To be happy. And to not think. That is dwelling — it will require strength. You are not self-destructive!

Clear your mind — the next moment is a new moment. Every moment is a new moment. How exciting.

Be blank and live.

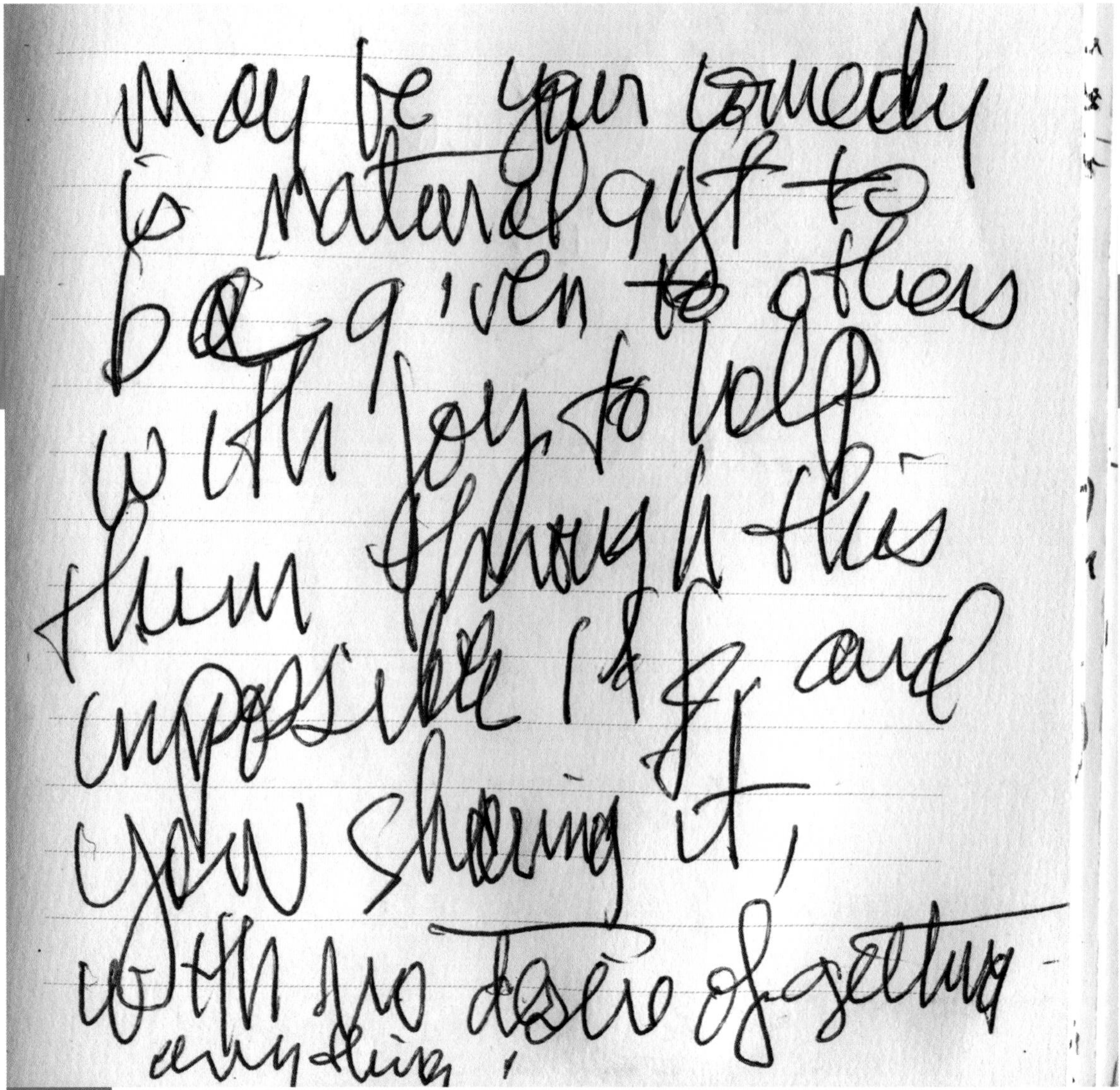

may be your comedy
is natural gift to
be given to others
with joy to help
them through this
impossible life and
you sharing it,
with no desire of getting
anything!

Garry Shandling in Progress

MEDITATE
EMPTY OUT
LET GO FROM
ALL CELLS

GARRY I used to say life is short, but not short enough.

Dec 13,
Heres some good
news: Everything
is impermanent and
has no reality
(empty).

GARRY The journals are all about understanding that this path you and I are talking about now is the most important thing in life. And that show business or anything else is secondary. So I started meditating at twenty-five, which is many, many, many years ago, and people were making fun of it. This is before there were Buddhas in windows in Beverly Hills, right? So I would go out and meditate.

Be unattached to
this life.
Be unattached to
your body.

Nothing is yours.

The ego desires.

Desire needs suffering.

Attachment needs suffering.

Awake! Nothing that
bothers you is real.

1990

DAVE COULIER I knew that he was very spiritual in a lot of ways. Back in the '80s he would go out to the desert or his cabin up at Big Bear and just kinda chill out in his own kinda Zen way. But, you know, it wasn't as if it was very pronounced. It wasn't like "Hey, excuse me, I gotta go do some Zen stuff right now."

JUDD 'Cause he said back then no one was doing it.

DAVE No one was. And he was into health foods. He had a health food store that he would go to. He was doing crystals. Not like crystal meth or anything. But—

JUDD The old crystals.

DAVE The old crystals. You know, the traditional crystals.

Let go - drop - all resistance, that is ego. Drop - let go - of all "stories," such as mother, show business, hard work, even spiritual path - that is ego. You are scared of awakening, Let go of that.

2004

BETH D'ANGELO (friend/personal trainer in Hawaii) I asked him why he had a circle on the back of his neck, and he said, "It's not a circle. Look closer." And he said, "It's an Ensō." And he went on to explain what it meant for him: that things don't have to always come to completion. It's the process. That Ensō meant a lot to Garry, because he would talk about the process of getting from this point to this point. That's where the intuition is, that's where the wisdom is, that's where you stumble and fall and you get back up.

The Ensō symbol appears again and again throughout Garry's journals, representing both emptiness and enlightenment and often accompanied by the invocation of the similar concept *mu*.

SARAH SILVERMAN I think he turned to Buddhism and really mastered it intellectually, but because he needed it. And there are so many people that need it and never know it and never explore it, but he was in constant practice. He had rage, he could really hold on to stuff and be troubled by things that to other people might seem small, but he was always working on that, always trying to process it and understand it. And I feel the same way: I can give great advice, but it's hard to see ourselves, because we don't have perspective. We're in us.

GARRY The world is too noisy and distracted to probably ultimately survive. Everyone needs to shut the fuck up. The answers are in the silence. Monks set themselves on fire to protest and to make this point. Just consider it.

ED SOLOMON He was always trying to find a way that the constant pain that he was in, and the constant no-self, could be turned into a positive. That's what his entire life was. And that's what Buddhism is. It's about the attainment of no-self. And it's incredibly ironic that he was at the center of these shows in such a gigantic way, but at the same time struggling to make peace with this idea that there was no self there. And to turn it positive. That's what the shows were too. *How do I take my struggle of identity and turn it into something positive?*

GARRY All the bad things happen in the mind, and yet most people live in their minds. But if you start listening to your head—and it takes such discipline, it's why you see monks meditate five times a day, because they're nothing but humans. So if they don't meditate that third time of the day, they could slip and say, "She's hot."

Oct 24
Let go of apparent
reality — these bodies,
minds, blood, muscles,
women, money, cars, houses,
desire, attachment, houses

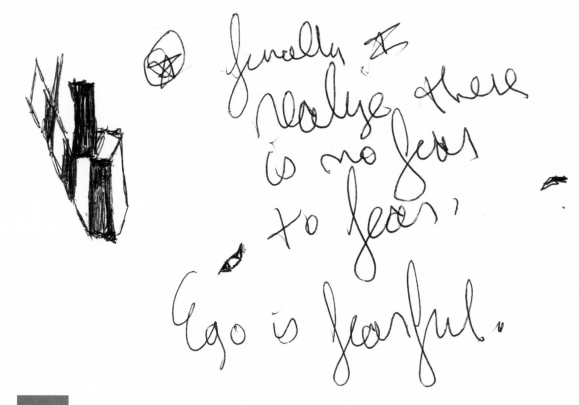

finally I
realize there
is no fear
to fear,

Ego is fearful.

2005

SARAH SILVERMAN They say if you worry about the past it's depression, and if you stress about the future it's anxiety, and that's why it's important to be in the moment, and no one knows that intellectually more than Garry because he was a Buddhist and he studied Buddhism. And that was what he put so much of his time and his love into, but it's not because he's Zen, it's because he was in desperate need of being Zen. So him toiling for eight months over a five-minute set goes against everything he studies and works so hard for and writes about in his journals, but that's why he needs it so badly.

GARRY I can meditate to the point where my mind is blank, but then there's no one to blame.

August .16
We can fix the world.

You will become an elder and accept it and embrace it. Ease into it. Be it. JOY, LOVE & FORGIVE JAY. HE IS Al Hazzen

Stay within yourself. Being
Let the fight come
to you. JOY JOY

Craig Kilborn. Love for Johnny.
Stay open. For the journey of life —
The message is in the presence — the emptiness,
the light altitude. Self-love for acceptance of your
We can fix the world death.

You don't need to be successful. You don't need to be funny or a good actor or writer. You don't need to be anything. You can just be.

GARRY All my journey is is to be authentically who I am. Not trying to be somebody else under all circumstances.

PAUL PROVENZA (comedian) Have you found confusion?

GARRY Sure. The whole world is confused because they're trying to be somebody else. To be your true self takes enormous work. Then we can start to look at the problems in the world. But instead, ego drives it. Ego drives the world. Ego drives the problem. So you have to work in an egoless way. This egolessness, which is the key to being authentic, is a battle. And it's a battle that has to be won before we're worried about the economy.

PAUL Do you think being a comic sort of stunts our growth in that direction?

GARRY I would say that I struggle to not have that happen. That's my struggle.

Let go of judgement. of others and of yourself. Forgive — INTEGRATE IT. OPEN. OPEN ALL PARTS OF BODY. TAKE IN CHI TO ALL PARTS. BREATH INTO ALL PARTS. OPEN. LET GO. HEAL BY BEING IN NOW. BREATH. MEDITATE. CONCENTRATE ON BREATH. STAY IN NOW. THE Relative ~~ABSOLUTE~~ REALITY IS A DREAM. YOU ARE NOT YOUR BODY. YOU ARE NOT YOUR MIND. IT IS AN ILLUSION. STAY EMPTY. BE PATIENT. NO RUSH TO GET INTO SHAPE. BE NEITHER IN SHAPE NOR OUT OF SHAPE. BE NOTHING. O

FORGIVE OTHERS.
THERE IS NO BLAME. IT IS
YOUR PROJECTION.
EGO IS THIS WORLD OF ILLUSION.
EGO IS ILLUSION.
EGO IS THE ILLUSION.
EGO IS THE FALSE SELF.

TRUST WHAT YOU WANT.

WHAT YOU DO IS AUTOMATICALLY
    RIGHT FOR THE OTHER PERSON,
  TRUST IN GOD, SPIRIT, THE
HIGHER POWER. SEPERATENESS IS AN
ILLUSION. GOD-I ASK FOR GUIDANCE.
I GIVE MYSELF UP TO YOU AND ASK
FOR FORGIVENESS. HELP ME BE
COMPASSIONATE. AND LOVING.

2006

Garry Shandling ✓
@GarryShandling

I hobbled today for the very first time -- it was for just a very, -- hair-split second. But it was a hobble. I'm sure of if.

Garry Shandling ✓
@GarryShandling

Attn Ncaa: I was funny enough in college to be paid.

Garry Shandling ✓
@GarryShandling

I'm starting to envy those who live under a dictatorship and don't have to vote.

#DemDebate

Garry Shandling ✓
@GarryShandling

I didn't get married, but I did get a participation trophy. So I feel pretty good about myself.

Garry Shandling ✓
@GarryShandling

I'm starting to look like Garry Shandling. I didn't see that coming.

Garry Shandling ✓
@GarryShandling

I am the best defensive back in the NFL. That's why I pat so many guys on the ass.

Garry Shandling ✓
@GarryShandling

The only UFOs we see are the ones that slow down for a moment to stare the way we all do when there's an accident on the side of road.

Garry Shandling ✓
@GarryShandling

I GET AN ENDORPHINE RUSH FROM USING THE CAPS LOCK.

ENLIGHTENMENT IN TWELVE ROUNDS

Not everyone can find inner awareness while taking a one-two combo to the gut, but Garry's search for spiritual self-abnegation led him into the boxing ring, where he traded punchlines for actual punches. Garry was such a devotee of the sweet science that he eventually opened his own gym, which he co-owned with director Peter Berg.

Relax, throw punches.

PETER BERG One of the things that we really love about boxing is
that when you get into that ring, there's no bullshit. Even if it's
horrible, ugly, sophomoric fighting, it's still fighting, and it takes
real courage to get into that ring and confront yourself. I think
obviously there's parallels to stand-up comedy, to the lifestyle that
Garry lived where he was very interested in peeling away all the
bullshit and finding out what was really lurking inside, and a
boxing ring is a good place to be exposed to that.

Garry Shandling in Progress

World Middleweight

Garry Shandling VS Himself

Championship

TEMPERED STEEL

GARRY Dave Duchovny called me up about ten years ago and he said, "Here's something that's gonna really push you out of your comfort zone." It gets very much like an acting workshop, because you have to be in the moment, and it's a scene. The punching and the getting punched has to be one.

KEVIN SMITH (director/writer) Explain.

GARRY As soon as you start to separate it, you're in your head. So you have your scene, you have your game plan, and you go in, and you clear your head. And it's a dance, and you can feel the other guy's intentions. You know, there's an old fight coach that says, "It's simple: It's hitting the other guy more." But, in fact, the core of it is, you've got to really know yourself. You can't fake it in the ring.

It's a very soul-searching, Zen kind of experience, 'cause you have somebody throwing punches at you and you have to transcend that, which is like transcending life and not thinking too much about the dangers all the time.

No mind.

Don't make anything a personal problem

THAT'S "THE STORY

Don't cope with reactive pattern

Like boxing – Be in the moment, take punches as the same as giving them, or just moving – meaning that once you go into the ring (this malevolestic body + life) you can't complain or be fearful of "punches" for they are inherent in the "ring" ~ life.

Feel love for yourself and — just feel love. that is it.

The mind cannot understand the present moment and/or the energy of living in Now, living in an emptiness. Don't expect your Mindself to understand — it shouldn't, because it can't.

2007

KEVIN This is a pussy question, but does it hurt when you get hit?

GARRY Well, my name in the gym is Garry "Not in the Face" Shandling.

KEVIN That was before you took up boxing as well, I believe.

GARRY Yeah, it was. In my sex life that was actually the warning that was given.

GARRY IN PARADISE

Like the boxing ring, Hawaii represented for Garry a spiritual refuge away from the demands and difficulties of real life—a place where he could feel at peace.

Let go of all past
"Garry Shandling" is
a body-name. A false
identity for purposes of
scyterie Reality. Let it
all go. Be willing to
reside in stillness, needing
nothing, wanting nothing,
beeing nothing ⊙.

Mother may die today.
same. For her: Let Go
~~for~~ For U, let go. Let go
of mother, all the
bullshit. ⊙

only Love for
the energy she
was. compassion
for the pain she could
not pull out of.

You are ◯

I'm Hawaii. How about
that? From the
earth back to earth.
Never Born; Never Die.

All anger and attitudes are
false self.
         ↓
STAY IN PRESENCE!
STAY IN ENERY of BODY

Develope Mindful patience
Let Go or watch anger be.

JUDD What did you think he got out of going to the Four Seasons on Kona? What did it mean to him?

BETH D'ANGELO (friend/personal trainer in Hawaii) I think that it was a place for Garry to unplug from his life and his creativity and a lot of what he was involved with on the mainland. I really didn't know the Garry that everybody else did. I got to meet Garry the laid-back guest who was working on strength and posture. And we really went into a lot of spiritual talking, and he felt very comfortable walking among those of us that worked there, and I think that he really liked that we knew him and we gave him space. I think he really embraced the rawness of being authentic, and us letting him be real because we were being real.

JUDD Where does Hawaii fit in in his spirituality? What was special about Hawaii to him?

BETH You can't drive your car, there's no traffic, it's not easily accessible. The Big Island, in my experience, is rooted in spirituality. The locals call it Pele's magic.

JUDD And did he talk to you about his childhood and his mom and his struggles with her?

BETH Well, before I knew anything about his mother, I had made a comment, something like "I hope your mother is extremely proud of who you are." And his body froze, and I immediately thought I'd just said something that I should not have, and he just let me know that his relationship with his mother was strained. He had lost his brother when he was younger. He was in therapy because of his mother. A lot of things came back to Mom.

He mentioned Barry I think just once, when he explained to me that Barry had died of cystic fibrosis. And I identified with that because I lost my son. And I remember Garry just stopping and looking at me and saying, "That's a tough one." And I said, "It is." I think I offered Garry a sense of what his mother could have been to him that she wasn't. And Garry showed me what it was like to stay in the game. I said to Garry very boldly, "You were the son that was left behind." And he said, "Yes, I was." It broke my heart. It helped launch me into realizing that I cannot have my other two sons, who are still here, feel like I was not available, and that's a gift that Garry gave me.

GARRY WITH THE ASSIST

Throughout his career, and especially during the last decades of his life, Garry relished his role as a comedy mentor, always willing to lend a hand in pursuit of a joke. His Sunday basketball games were a storied nexus for some of Hollywood's funniest people, and a place where he could spend time with the friends and colleagues he'd gathered as a family.

Become old Gracefully,
Become a mentor gracefully

JON FAVREAU He had the kind of impact where I thought I had a special relationship with him because he was a bit of a mentor. I would show him my scripts, I would show him cuts of my movie. He would make the time for me. And then you realize that there are dozens of people who felt this deep connection to the guy, a whole generation of people coming up, and how generous he was with his time.

SARAH SILVERMAN He was so generous. It was hilarious to me just how supportive he was when I would get emails from him like "I saw you on *The Joy Behar Show* on Headline News network, really good stuff, you were so honest and in the moment." I didn't hear from my mother for those things.

Garry Shandling in Progress

Notes Garry wrote in 2005 for the movie *The 40-Year-Old Virgin*.

SACHA BARON COHEN (actor) I always hoped in England that I would meet a bunch of comedians who would kind of mentor me and say, "This joke isn't really working for this reason." It never happened in England. In England, there were these smaller fiefdoms. Everyone had their group of writers. They held on to them and they didn't really collaborate. And then I came here, and there was suddenly this guy who was helping me out. For no money and no credit, and he had no desire for thanks, and I never really understood it. I'd always say, "Can I pay you, or can I give you a credit?" And he never wanted it. He was like this comic angel. He was the comic fairy godmother.

413

After Garry's passing, friends gathered at his house to play one last game of basketball.

SARAH SILVERMAN If you go to his basketball games there are a lot of celebrities, exciting people you want to see. But there are writer's assistants, there are struggling comedians, struggling writers, people who haven't figured it out yet, and there was no hierarchy in his mind. Everyone was potential.

I lived for Sundays. I started when I was twenty-four, and now I'm forty-six. Good twenty years, a solid twenty years of Sundays, although there were boyfriends here and there where I skipped a bunch, maybe years' worth in a row. I think people scoff or laugh and assume he's not an athlete, but he was. He was a really good basketball player, and he went on to box and do all that shit. I think he loved the camaraderie. There's nothing I love more than hanging out with a bunch of comics. There's the common goal of playing games of basketball to 7:00 P.M., but it's mostly bits and laughing, and it's pure joy. We all called it Camp Garry.

KEVIN NEALON There were a lot of injuries. I think Billy Crystal twisted his leg.

SACHA BARON COHEN Once he died, I put out this basketball net in memory of him, and we had all these guys who were playing basketball at his house with nowhere to play. And so now they've been playing basketball at my house. And I remember the first night we played, and it was great we all got together, but it was just so quiet. Because we realized how many one-liners he'd shout out from the sidelines.

GARRY Let me assure you—and this isn't a joke—the older I get, the more often I think of "Are we there yet?" It's like if you were on a car trip going across the country or something and as you get closer you can sense that you're getting closer.

417

DAVID DUCHOVNY He kind of had a smoke screen about whatever his health was. None of us really knew what was going on with Garry physically at any time.

BILL ISAACSON There was this underlying thing for several years of him being concerned that he didn't feel that well. And then he was diagnosed with hyperparathyroidism and later pancreatitis, which made him foggy and feel an aging that did not make sense to Garry. He had major surgery for pancreatitis. They opened him up and were in there for six hours. He was in the hospital for most of a week. He was really scared, but in the same way talking to himself and connecting it to his spirituality: "I can do this, I can love people, I can get through this, I can recognize my fear." But he was also, you know, so private.

SARAH SILVERMAN I didn't know when he was in the hospital for like three weeks and there was a calcium weird thing and all that stuff. I didn't even know about it. And then when I found out about it I got really upset in a way that I hadn't experienced with him. I was so angry, I felt angry at him and I felt so upset, and I remember calling him and saying, like, "Who's your emergency contact if I'm not your emergency?" Because I need to know that somebody is, because I thought of him just being alone. He wasn't good at reaching out and needing help, and for me he was such a caretaker.

Well, the time has come. My pancreatitis requires surgery.

Poker face. Accept. Be!

2014

419

GARRY You know, I've been meditating for thirty-five years so I can meditate until my mind is pretty empty, pretty blank. But then there's no one to blame. (*Ram Dass laughs*) Now I realize I have an audience for my meditation material.

RAM DASS Humor is great in the spiritual work. You must know that. It gets you there.

GARRY Humor comes from an objective place, which is where the meditation is: the silence. Everything becomes objective. People who aren't funny, or don't have a sense of humor, they are not in the moment. That's why they are not humorous. They're constantly in here (*points to his head*) so they take everything literally.

RAM DASS I'd say in here (*points to his heart*), not here (*points to his head*). Here is serious. Here is the judge. Here is the yuck. And, down here (*points to heart*), there's really humor down here, the humor of wisdom.

When Garry interviewed Jerry Seinfeld for the *Larry Sanders* DVD extras, it planted the germ of an idea in Seinfeld's head that would eventually lead to the creation of his own free-flowing interview series *Comedians in Cars Getting Coffee*. Seinfeld later returned the favor by inviting his old friend to be a guest on the show.

SULI MCCULLOUGH (comedian) Garry asked me to help him get ready for *Comedians in Cars*. For him, it was about the relationship—his relationship with Jerry. The fact that they hadn't spoken in a long time. He knew that's what this was about. And the jokes were a part of that, but first and foremost it was about the relationship.

JERRY SEINFELD You know David Brenner passed away last year. All that material, he worked so hard on it. It's gone. It doesn't mean anything to anyone anymore. It took so much work to create it.

GARRY That material and your material is purely a vehicle for you to express your spirit and your soul and your being and that's why you're fantastic. So you keep—

JERRY So it doesn't have any value beyond that?

GARRY It doesn't have any value beyond you expressing yourself in a very soulful, spiritual way. It's why you're on the planet!

Garry Shandling in Progress

GAVIN DE BECKER In the last couple of years we talked a lot about death, and if I can be so— It doesn't matter; he was ready. Garry was ready. We can be sad for ourselves; we have little reason to be sad for Garry. We talked about it a lot and I am quite persuaded from emails and texts and a million conversations that he was okay with this, as we all better be. Before a very serious surgery last year when we knew he could die at the surgery, Garry asked me to sign those papers to be the person who could decide to disconnect life support systems if it came to that, and we discussed his wishes in detail, including when to pull the plug, and at some point he said to me, "Don't do it if I'm sitting up in the bed yelling, 'Don't do it!'"

JIM CARREY We'd talk about death. We talked about death a lot. And I noticed in him, like, a surrender to whatever was. There was this feeling of a slowed cadence, and I didn't know there was something physical— I actually asked Jimmy about it. I said, "Garry seems to be speaking very haltingly." He really had a beautiful focus on life and on spirituality. He seemed to be kind of an awakened person. I'd been on that path myself, so we had a lot to share. And it was wonderful. But I was concerned. He would speak and take breaths in the middle of sentences. And his cadence had changed. And I didn't know whether it was because he had given up that character or that he was actually struggling to get breath. I thought, *If he wants to hang out with me every night, he's probably ready.*

If you live another 3 weeks, be grateful. If you live another 3 years, be grateful.

2014

Death is not a change.
Embrace Death. It is freedom—
even Nothing. Be open, be
ready, be joyful to die. 🌀
And Life and death are no two,
So in life be willing to make a bad
choice and die.
Like a warrior - willing and
ready at each moment to die

Accept the outside world.

Stewardess asked
me, "Do people in Hollywood
retire?" I've gone from
young comedian to this.
Reading old journal I
see how I succeeded
in growing into
me on stage. Now I need
to grow into me in life. ✦
✦ Your burden is no more
than others - less than
many. Be authentic in
life.

Heal and don't forget
gratitude just to
be. Gratitude for
others, and for the
earth and sky
and "life." Acceptance.

May 14
Aaron Hernandez of
N.E. Patriots is in jail
for 3 Homicides.
You are in Hawaii.

This moment,
only.

2014

The *Larry Sanders Show* cast back together in 2012 for *Entertainment Weekly*'s "Reunions" issue.

It's Official: 'The Larry Sanders Show' Coming to HBO Go and HBO Now in September

Photofest
'The Larry Sanders Show'

f 𝕏

All six seasons of the comedy will be available on HBO Go and HBO Now beginning Sept. 23.

The Larry Sanders Show is finally coming to HBO Go—in September

William Hughes
7/30/16 3:49pm

Garry Shandling in Progress

BILL ISAACSON The day he passed away, I'm in a legal proceeding. I'm at a break and I get an email from his business person saying they sold *Larry Sanders* last night to HBO. And I thought, *Oh, that's great, that's really like a nice piece of news. That's what Garry had really wanted the last couple months.* And then a couple hours later I got an email saying, "You have to call. Your friend is not gonna make it." And it was remarkable that the night before he passed, that that was finally done.

MARTIN LESAK (Garry's agent) Garry had gotten on with me and said, "It'd be great if [*The Larry Sanders Show*] could live at HBO. That's where I'd want it to be." I coincidentally was having a breakfast with those guys and I brought up the show and they both had said, just like that, "Are you kidding? HBO wouldn't be HBO without that show. That show defined our network. It's everything to us. Of course we want it to live here."

Ultimately, we all forced it through and they figured out how to get the deal done, and strangely enough, the deal closed the night before Garry passed away. And I tried to get him that night. I was leaving a taping and I called him at I think nine-thirty, ten, and I didn't get him, which for some bizarre reason kind of concerned me. I could usually get him. He was usually there in the evenings. That was the time I could really get on the phone with him and have a conversation with him about whatever. And I didn't get him, and I thought, *Oh, I hope he's okay.* And then, on my way in, my assistant called me in the car and said, at nine-thirty the next morning, somewhere thereabouts, "Garry's on the line." And I jumped on, and I was like, "Garry!" I was my crazy self, and he was like, "Hey, did, did the deal close?" And I said, "Yes, it closed," and he said, "Hey, Martin, you know I don't feel well. I don't feel well."

Then I said, "Well, what, what's wrong?" And he said, "I have this horrible pain in my lower back and in my leg," and I said, "Like how bad? Like kidney stone bad?" And he said, "Oh, this is far worse than a kidney stone," and I said, "Garry, should I come pick you up?" Like, "You need to get to a doctor now?" And he said, "Well, I have a friend coming to pick me up," who was his driver who he referred to as his friend, which I loved. "I'm headed to UCLA, and it'll all be good. But thank you so much for getting this closed. I'm so happy. You've made my day." And that was it. I got the call an hour later that he was on his way to the hospital from his driver, and he said, "It's not good, this is really bad." I was like, "What do you mean it's really bad? I was just talking to him." He's like, "This is really bad." And that was, that was the end.

KEVIN NEALON He wasn't feeling well, and he was going to go to the doctor but he couldn't get his car service or something, so instead of calling an Uber he said, "I'll wait until tomorrow." And he waited too long. The driver was waiting for him outside. He called the driver and said he was running behind a little bit. He was getting dressed. And then I guess he came downstairs and started, I would imagine, feeling the heart attack coming on and called 911. And then they arrived and had to climb over the fence and, I guess, break in and try to revive him. But it was too late. You can't imagine what he's going through that last moment like that. You know, just sheer panic. Even after all these thoughts in the journal and stuff, you know, it's just you have that—most of us have that, just that strong willingness to survive and to live, you know, and I think he had a lot of life ahead of him. I think he was finally coming up with answers. You know, he seemed very . . . relaxed with life. Accepting.

JUDD Maybe he had enough answers to let go. A lot of what he wrote in these journals when he was going into these surgeries were things like, "You have to be okay with dying. It's okay if you live three days. It's okay if you live three months. Just let go."

KEVIN That's all fine philosophically speaking, but when it's actually happening, you know, it's like getting on a roller coaster.

JUDD His last text was to his driver. He said, "It's going to be a weird day today."

KEVIN I think when he said it was going to be a weird day, it was weird for us, not so much him. It was weird because we are the ones that have to kind of process it and accept it.

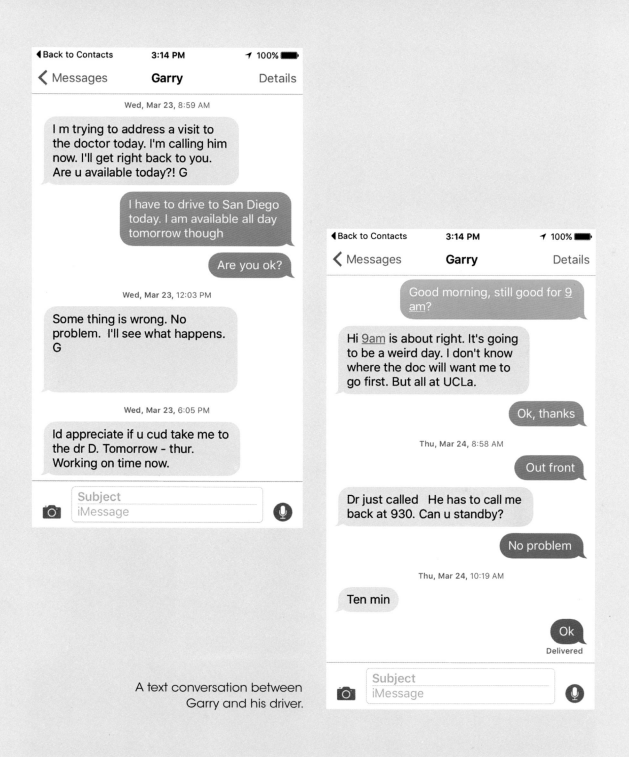

A text conversation between
Garry and his driver.

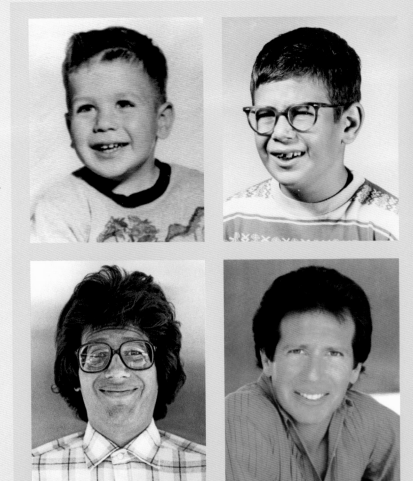

THANK YOU, GARRY

Garry died unexpectedly from pulmonary thrombosis on March 24, 2016. One month later, a group of his friends, family members, collaborators, and admirers held a memorial for him commemorating his life in the most appropriate way possible: a night of copious jokes and self-deprecating honesty.

ABOVE: (top, left to right): Don Was, Jon Brion, and Adam Sandler, (bottom) Adam Sandler
NEXT PAGE: (top) Penny Johnson and Jeffrey Tambor, (bottom) Mark Oliver Everett

Thank You, Garry

JUDD APATOW It's odd that Prince just died, because Garry and Prince were very similar. They really were no different, because when you really get down to it, Garry was the Prince of comedy. He was mysterious, complicated, sexually ambiguous. His talent endless. He was a brilliant performer who may or may not have been high the entire time. He had great hair. Both stood up against the man to get their shit back. And both were sexy as a mother-fucker. *The Larry Sanders Show* was Garry's *Purple Rain*. *It's Garry Shandling's Show* was his *Dirty Mind*. The only difference between the two men was that Garry had a huge cock. That is the joke that Garry would have wanted and we know that.

SARAH SILVERMAN You know what I like to do after I masturbate? Speak at a nice memorial service. I stole that joke from Garry Emmanuel Shandling. He was my mentor, my friend, support system, family, he was a caregiver, all of those. He was the most generous man I knew. Generous with his knowledge, with his mind—all the things that he learned the hard way he offered to me wrapped up in a bow. And there are so many of us here tonight that can say that. He made us feel so loved and supported and mirrored with the best lighting. He gave with his whole being. He was the giving tree.

For years all the furniture in my apartment was from his storage unit. And I still have a lot of it today, plus a bunch of towels. Garry taught me about acting, about comedy and about life, and patience and honesty, and the bravery in being vulnerable, the importance of the empty spaces, the pauses, the gold in between the words.

I guarded him every Sunday in basketball for about eighteen of the twenty-one years I knew him. Sundays were pure joy. My favorite day, the summer camp I never knew. And all of us from basketball at Camp Garry know each other through Garry and we are forever friends. He is the glue between so many friendships in this town. He loved life. He, at the very least, liked life.

I can say with total confidence and truly not because of any romance of this heart-breaking circumstance that at least one-third of everything I am, the best parts of me, are a direct result of Garry Shandling. When my mother died in August, he comforted me with a Buddhist expression that went "Grief, teach me what I have to learn." And what I've learned from grief is that she is a strange mistress who works in jagged, inconsistent, unpredictable ways. You may want to cry when you find out your close friend is gone, but grief says, "Nah, I'm going to go ahead and wait until you're in line at Gelson's in two weeks." Like my mind knows that he is gone but my body and my bones are positive that he's just in Hawaii. I am the exact age Garry was when I met him. And I hope to pass on to the young comics I meet just some of the lessons he taught me—not all of them, because I still need to have that edge.

I wish he felt—I hope he felt—as loved and cared for and thought of and supported as he made all of us feel. And I know he will live through the almost unimaginable amount of people he has so profoundly touched. I love you, Garry. Thank you, and I love all of you.

437

BILL ISAACSON Garry and I were close friends. We loved one another and trusted one another. One of the ways I knew Garry was as a writer. And he has left us more. He has left us notes, files, piles, journals, and more legal pads and legal paper than any lawyer I know, scattered throughout. Paper plates. This is part of his legacy. A legacy of spirituality and comedy that's going to take years to process. This was Garry thirty years ago: "July 7, 1986. Instead of trying not to die, decide how you want to live. If this was your last week, how would you live? How do you want to lead your life? A life of spiritual growth, a happy life to have the self-esteem to confront. Sorry, just killed a spider."

BRUCE GRAYSON He loved that Sunday game. The guys and Sarah had showed up to play a little three-on-three, tell some jokes, laugh, and watch sports. The game was sacred to Garry. A place where people could leave troubles behind and just be. Many nights after the games ended Garry would be found huddled down in conversation with one of them who had asked for his help or advice. He compassionately challenged friends to dig deeper, try harder, and find the courage to make tough decisions. He did it all with deep love. At his core he was a teacher: Dr. Garry, the professor of life. He was fascinated by the human condition, what motivated people, how the ego was the root of all problems, how it prevented us from making instinctive decisions. For Garry it was always about the work, reaching down deep to your core and rolling around in a painful place for as long as it took to live an authentic life.

GAVIN DE BECKER One time I was on a book tour, the third book tour in a row, and I hated my book and I hated myself, and I hated the questions and I hated my answers and I was exhausted and I called Garry and I asked for advice and he said, "You just go and do the show and remember that you never know what's coming." And I argued with him and I said, "I know exactly what's coming, it's a radio call-in show. I know exactly what they're going to ask and I know exactly what I'm going to say." He said, "Go do the show." And so I did, and the third caller on the radio call-in show said, "Am I on the air?" And fuck, it was Garry's voice. And so I sat up and paid attention and, you know, I'm there to do my serious blah blah blah about preventing violence and all of that, and the host says, "Caller, do you have a question for Mr. de Becker?" And the caller says, "Are you the same Gavin de Becker that used to beat me up in the fourth grade?" And—true story—for the rest of that book tour, no joke, I came back to life and I knew that anything could happen, so I started paying attention. And Garry forced me and a lot of you to be in the present moment, maybe forced millions of people to be in the present moment, because you didn't know what was coming.

Thank You, Garry

KEVIN NEALON The truth is I think it was very hard to be Garry. He was complex, at times neurotic, persnickety, high maintenance, a perfectionist with the highest standards, and he could be a handful. Being in his company required extra patience. I think the fact that he spelled his name with two r's was a warning that he was going to be complicated. I don't know why he creates that much trouble for himself. And Garry could never fully commit. He never could, and it drove a lot of us crazy. You know, we'd invite him to an event or a party or something, and there'd be a lot of hemming and hawing and second-guessing and doubting, and then came the stipulations. If he went, he could only stay for five minutes because he may have somewhere to go maybe after that or where he'd maybe have to be, but eventually I learned that was his process. That was Garry's dance and I came to expect that, and of course he always came, he showed up. And after he passed, my wife and I were going through some photos of different parties and events that we had or we went to, and Garry was at all of them. And he was usually looking at the exit. And Garry sometimes preferred it to be all about him. And I saw that. When my wife was pregnant we had a coed baby shower only because Garry showed up. Not really, but we had a contest to come up with the best baby name, and Garry's submission was Garry Emmanuel Shandling Nealon. And he went home with the trophy on that one. It took some work to be Garry's friend, but it was so, so worth it. I mean, he was quality. He was the gold standard.

I loved our conversations on the phone. I miss those: late into the night, talking about comedy and joke structure. It was just him and me—and, on occasion, Anthony Pellicano. Garry was so brilliant in so many ways, and so inspiring, and having his approval meant the world to me. And of course his friendship meant more. I loved Garry for everything he was. And I don't know how I'll ever stop missing him, and I don't care to stop missing him. I read somewhere that grief is not a sign of weakness. Grief is just the price you pay to love someone, and I could tell you that Garry was very, very expensive. And that fucker bankrupted me.

On February 4, 2019, friends and family of Garry's gathered together at the David Geffen School of Medicine at the UCLA Medical Center to celebrate the opening of the Garry Shandling Learning Studio, named in honor of a $15.2 million endowment gifted by Garry to the school. The funds will establish and endow the Garry Shandling Endocrine Surgery Research Fund, the Garry Shandling Infectious Diseases Innovation Fund, and the Garry Shandling Pancreatic Diseases Fund.

DR. KELSEY MARTIN (dean of the David Geffen School of Medicine) Garry Shandling's contribution will enhance the innovative research being undertaken by our exceptional team of physicians and scientists. His generosity will ensure that we have the resources to pursue promising therapies to dramatically improve our patients' quality of life.

Thank You, Garry

Photos Garry took of a poem written
by Maynard Dixon in 1935.

SANCTUARY

Lonely— lonely & vast . . . .
this is the ultimate peak & the outlook—
here begins the long release & the silence—
here the trail ends.

The good horse is tired now:
throw the reins down,
take the bit from his mouth,
tie up the bridle snug to the saddle-horn.
Turn the horse loose;
he will leisurely find his way
back to the home corral in the quiet evening.

Come on then, you buzzards,—
only a little while it will take for you to find me.
The wide & pitiless circling,
the long & slowly descending glide
of your dark & darkness-confirming wings
to me shall be welcome.

Come on, buzzards, make a clean job.
Tear the old garments away—
the outworn ridiculous garments, these, of my life—
tear them away.
Pick the bones clean—
Leave nothing small or unworthy—
let them lie free in the rain, free to the
    white-cleansing sun.
leave only my thoughts.
These thoughts that once made me a man
surely will find their way
back to the home corral in the quiet evening.

A LETTER TO BARRY

After Garry's death, a letter was found addressed to his late brother, Barry. Penned in 2005, forty-five years after Barry's passing, this raw and heartfelt message reveals just how much the event continued to impact Garry all those years later.

Dear Barry,
You died during the night. My hunch is that you were a special spirit...Blessed and cursed with a disease. What you went through. Could I have understood then? I saw your pain and coughing during the night. Did we ever talk about it? I would guess not. Seeing how much denial Mother had when Dad died, I can't imagine any other way.

You must have been strong to do so much of it alone. I remember Dad crying to perhaps another man, "We've lost him." It's the only real, honest moment I recall. That I didn't speak to you at the end. Or sit there as you passed is something

I apologize for. Nor did I do it with Dad. Nor Grandma. Mother kept saying, "they are fine," but yet I knew better and didn't push my way past her. This has been one of my "life" battles.

So I say to you—I have been holding in sadness for you. And for Dad. At least I was able to cry at his funeral. For you, I couldn't even go the funeral. Any real look at death—or as mom put it, "I didn't want you to see me crying"— wasn't seen fit for someone

who had been
born 10 years prior.
Seems to me that
a good time. Instead
I locked it up. Shut-down.
become aware of life-
death and time passage
and was in such pain
that I was taken to
the doctor where he
said, "there's nothing
physically wrong." My

emotional pain was
immense. that is
how much I
missed you, and
how sad I was, and
yet no way to
express it, whether
through prayer, funeral,
some other ceremony,
my communication -
No one to put their hand
on my shoulder, nod
and say, "Ahhh."

As you passed - a
little boy like
me doesn't know
where he stops
and his brother
picks up. So when
you died, I died.
Or a piece. It went
with you. So as
I dissolve that boundary
between you and I

that energy that
went is the
energy that is
sad. To unite
and see you all
again open up to
this light, your
light and my light.
I claim victory
for you, for me and
for us. love.
was never fully expressed

I express.
That abandonment
was a was something
I could only
deal with by
Splittingoff. Then
parent abandoned
me. No one to be
with me. No them
with me. And
then finally, no me

So Barry, I tell
you that I love
you. You were/are
joy. Now and
another time, we
will play together
and I will know
you as a "brother."
No wonder I felt
pain. You ripped
away. At your time,
A the deep abandonment and

missing you. And
being alone in
that house without
a "brother", without
you. To stay in
my body and feel
the pain. Okay and
true. And the love.
Good-bye from your this
world. Goodbye from the
pain of your body.
I honor your life, what a
special, short life, to
affect me so severly for so
long. Thank you. See you
on the other side. I love you.

Happy Holidays
from the
Shandling Family

Nov 1, 1989

Dear Garry,

40? You?

Look - it doesn't

hurt a bit.

Many Happy Returns.

If you make another

White House tour - holler; upstairs

Gz Bush

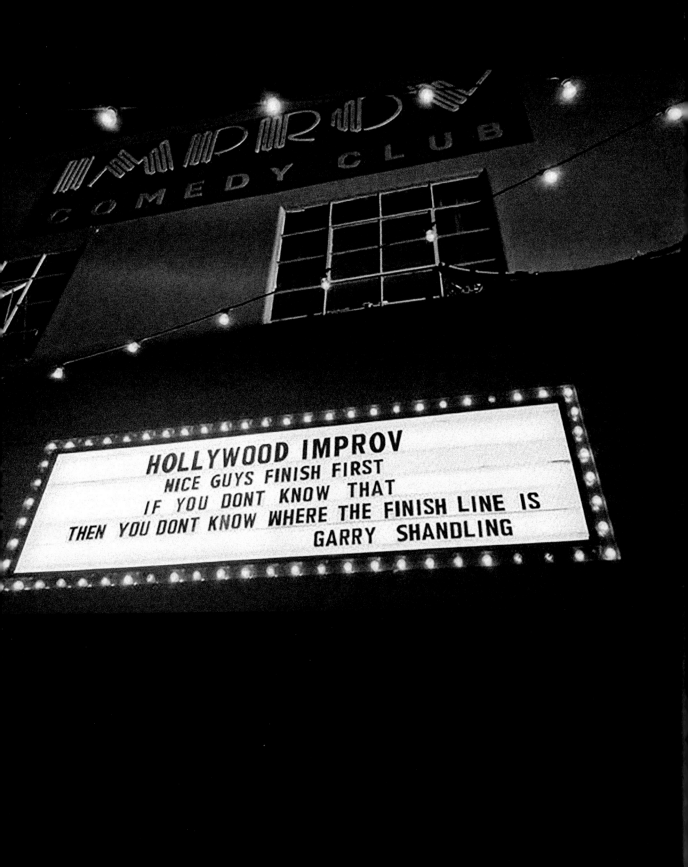

SOURCES

The vast majority of interviews in this book were conducted by Judd Apatow. In addition, here is a list of sources we drew from for further material in Garry's voice.

IN PRINT

Hirschberg, Lynn. "Garry Shandling Goes Dark." *The New York Times Magazine,* May 31, 1998.

Kronke, David. "Why Isn't This Man Smiling?" *Los Angeles Times,* August 27, 1995.

Martel, Jay. "Garry Shandling: True Lies." *Rolling Stone,* September 8, 1994.

"Playboy Interview: Garry Shandling." *Playboy,* December 1994.

"20 Questions: Garry Shandling." *Playboy,* July 1987.

AUDIO AND VIDEO

Alan King: Inside the Comedy Mind, 1991.

Archive of American Television interview with John Dalton. June 9, 2011.

"An Evening with Garry Shandling." William S. Paley Television Festival, February 29, 2000.

Fresh Air with Terry Gross, May 7, 2007.

Garry Shandling unpublished interview with Robert Lloyd.

The Pauly Shore Podcast Show. Episode 3, February 4, 2015.

SModcast with Kevin Smith. Episode 349, March 28, 2016.

WTF with Marc Maron. Episode 177, May 23, 2011.

You Made It Weird with Pete Holmes. Episode 299, January 13, 2016.

IMAGE CREDITS

Grateful acknowledgments are made to the following photographers and photo sources who graciously contributed their images to this book. Except for those specified below, all images are used courtesy of the Garry Shandling Estate.

ABOUT JUDD APATOW

Judd Apatow is one of the most important comic minds of his generation. He wrote and directed the films *The 40-Year-Old Virgin* (co-written with Steve Carell), *Knocked Up, Funny People,* and *This Is 40;* he directed *Trainwreck;* and his producing credits include *Superbad, Bridesmaids,* and *Anchorman.* Apatow was also the executive producer of the TV series *Freaks and Geeks,* HBO's *Girls* and *Crashing,* and *Love* on Netflix. In addition, he co-created the Emmy Award–winning television program *The Ben Stiller Show.* He is the author of *Sick in the Head* and editor of the collection *I Found This Funny.* Apatow lives in Los Angeles with his wife, Leslie Mann, and their two daughters, Maude and Iris.

FACEBOOK.COM/JUDDAPATOWOFFICIAL
TWITTER: @JUDDAPATOW
INSTAGRAM: @JUDDAPATOW